FOR THE ONE

Hope for the one who feels like giving up.

Much love,
EKWells

E . K . W E L L S

WESTBOW
P R E S S®
A DIVISION OF THOMAS NELSON
& ZONDERVAN

WestBow Press books may be ordered through booksellers or by contacting:

WestBow Press
A Division of Thomas Nelson & Zondervan
1663 Liberty Drive
Bloomington, IN 47403
www.westbowpress.com
844-714-3454

Scripture taken from the King James Version of the Bible.

ISBN: 978-1-6642-7581-2 (sc)
ISBN: 978-1-6642-7580-5 (hc)
ISBN: 978-1-6642-7582-9 (e)

Library of Congress Control Number: 2022915263

Print information available on the last page.

WestBow Press rev. date: 9/22/2022

DISCLAIMER

Each story is based on a true story and event that has taken place. To protect relationships that have been mended, names have been changed. Every story is told in the first person from the individual sharing their story. This is to keep the book authentic. The author has edited the stories to help keep the flow of the book. The author asked each individual, "What one word describes God throughout your story?" and their answer is the title of their story. *For the One* contains descriptive stories of abuse, addiction, and violence that may trigger readers who have been through similar situations.

If at any time you feel the Holy Spirit conviction to get saved, you can turn to the last page of the book for guidance.

DEDICATION

To the ones who put their darkest moments on paper for others to read, thank you. Thank you for your courage and faith in Christ that He will use your story to reach the ones.

To the ones reading this book: I was one of you. And I pray that in these pages, you find the unconditional love of Jesus Christ and accept Him as your Lord and Savior.

ACKNOWLEDGMENTS

To my heavenly Father, thank You for choosing me to write this book. Thank You for transforming me during the process of writing and never leaving my side when I doubted or ran from this calling. I will forever be grateful for this opportunity and this book.

Mom and Dad, thank you for teaching me that I can do anything with God's help. Thank you for never doubting that I could finish this book!

Rip and Ivy, thank you for not only being my family, but being my friends. Thank you both for being two people I can trust with my fears, my dreams, and everything in between. Thank you for letting me hang out at your house with those beautiful kids when life just seemed too heavy to go on.

Pawpaw Kennedy, although you didn't get to see the finished product, you were so proud of me and supportive of this book. Thank you for having the hard, uncomfortable conversation about our story and for giving me permission to share our story of redemption. I'm so thankful that through Christ, we were able to make peace before you passed. I am also grateful God gave us a couple of years with you after years of brokenness.

Grandma Kennedy, thank you for never giving up and always fighting for our relationship.

Grandma and Grandpa Jones, thank you for loving us so well

when it seemed like our world got turned upside down. You'll never know how much the two of you mean to me.

Editors, thank you for challenging me to become the best author I could be and helping me bring this book to life through these pages.

Designer, I may never have the words to express my gratitude for bringing my vision and heart for this book to life on the front cover. Thank you.

INTRODUCTION

Have you ever felt lost and all alone? When we enter this world, we have no control over the situation we are born into or the family we get. If we are lucky, we start out with a pretty good life. We're loved, protected, and provided for. But this isn't the case for everyone. For some individuals, the unimaginable actions of themselves or others lead to deep, unshakable heartache and pain. They self-destruct in an effort to escape, to find something to simply hold on to.

Yet in the middle of this brokenness, some find a miraculous peace that surpasses all understanding. They find extraordinary love through Jesus Christ. These are their stories—stories about hope for the hopeless, a Father for the fatherless, love for the unlovable, grace for the alcoholic, safety for the homeless, enough for the loss, redemption for the porn addict, freedom for the one imprisoned by his thoughts, forgiveness for the one longing to overcome a struggle, and identity for the one looking for approval.

The truth is we never know what people have been through or what they are currently experiencing. We may not ever hear their stories or know their scars. However, when we share our story, strangers become friends. People go from death to life. And in this book, we share our stories with you. My dear friend, you are loved. God loves you so much that He sent His Son, Jesus Christ, to die on the cross for you and your sins (John 3:16–17). Whether you are on the streets, in a church pew, or somewhere in between, God has a purpose for your life. He loves you right where you are.

We have poured our hearts out to you, and I pray you take in every word we share. As you open this book and read each story, you may feel the need to set the book down because a story touches your heart or hits a little too close to home. That's okay. Lean into that moment. Each soul has shared a story to reach you, the one reading this book. I ask that you open your heart and let God speak to you, change you, and bring you into a relationship with Him and a deeper understanding of Him. God sees you, loves you, and is reaching out to you just as you are. You don't have to be perfect or get your life in order to accept Christ today.

You may not relate to one person's entire story, but I do believe you can relate to one part of one person's story. Each story is all about Jesus – a love that leaves the ninety-nine for the one – and He rejoices when the one turns to Him (Luke 15:3-7). Friend, this book is for you, and we welcome you to read through each of our stories. May you see Christ in every page.

CONTENTS

FATHER

Father ∎

This is the untold story of a daughter and her son. Despite abuse,
torture, and rape, lives are saved in the midst of it all. They
are given the strength to stand tall. Where did it all go wrong?
This is the story of a loving Father that needs to be told.

My story isn't an easy one to tell. In fact, I have only told it in full three times. The first time I fainted. The second time I had a panic attack. The third time I was able to make it through the entire narrative. Each time I tell the story, I remember a little bit more, and it usually takes me some time to recuperate, to heal, and to rest. My therapist told me this is a normal reaction for those who have been through severe tragedy or multiple tragedies. Our brains repress the really big scary stuff. It's a coping mechanism for survival, and the best way to unlock those memories is to tell them. I am blessed each time I tell my story because God gives me more and more strength to overcome.

As I share my story today, my hope is that you will see God in His glory woven throughout every high mountaintop and the lowest of valleys. My prayer is that as you read with me, you will allow the Holy Spirit to show you the amazing things He has done throughout my life because of my experiences. May this bring hope and peace to you, and may you always remember God's word in Romans 8:28 (KJV): "And we know that all things work together for

3

good to them that love God, to them that are called according to his purpose." It says "all things," folks—the good, the bad, and the ugly.

Throughout my own life's story, as I reflect on the past, I can see clearly how God worked out each and every instance for good. And I hope you will see it too. Before I shared my testimony with my friend Elizabeth, she told me that God revealed the following to her: "You can't have a story without a beginning and an end." With that in mind, I start the beginning of my story with my earliest memory.

I was told the very first memory as far back as you can remember is supposed to define how your life goes. Well, if that were true, I would be in big trouble. Luckily, there is no truth to that. My first memory was when I was six years old. I remember being in a bathtub with my brother. My mom was washing us and frantically packing a bag at the same time. I didn't know what was going on except that she said we were leaving my dad. The next thing I knew, we were at my maternal grandmother's house. Surprisingly, my father showed up in a dangerous state.

Although my mom had placed my brother and me in Grandma's bedroom, we could see the living room and front door. My grandmother was holding us against her so our ears would be covered. Unfortunately for me, I kept my eyes open, and I could also hear everything that was going on. Because my grandmother wouldn't let my dad see us, he banged on the door, screaming and cursing. Paint and glass went everywhere when he chucked a can of red paint through the window. He found an axe and started to beat down the front door, tearing holes in it with every hit. My grandma went to call the police while my grandpa grabbed his gun. He stood at the door waiting for my dad to break through. The police showed up and took my dad away. That was my earliest memory. I found out later that was my dad's fourth felony, which meant he was looking at life in prison.

At the start of 1996, I was six years old, and it was right after Christmas. It was a good Christmas: my dad was home. Apparently, he was out on bond or something. The heat in our house went out all of a sudden, so we had to go to our neighbor's house to spend the night. We grabbed blankets and pillows, just thinking the heat was out.

I shared a bed with Dad, and I will never forget waking up and looking out the window over Dad's sleeping head. I could see our house was on fire. After I woke up my family, Dad grabbed the oldest of the neighbor's kids. They both ran into the burning house as we stood on the lawn, screaming, not knowing what would happen. The moments they were in the fire felt like hours, but they made it safely out of the house. The next day, we went through the ashes of what was left in our home. Later in life, I heard conflicting stories about that. Either they ran into the house to retrieve photo albums or to make it seem like an accident. We have no photos of us as kids, so they didn't save the albums.

It wasn't until I was sixteen that my aunt explained everything to me, and I understood what actually happened that day. My aunt explained that my dad was looking at life in prison, so he decided to burn our house down to get insurance money. Apparently, he had left a candle burning close to a curtain in the house, which caused the conflagration.

After the house burned down, we shared different family members' homes. We even lived in a hotel for a little while. Three months later, I went to bed in a hotel room and woke up surprised in Grandma's house. Mom told us Dad was gone. Thinking she meant he went to jail, we knew he would come back. However, Mom said he had died of a heart attack. Later, my aunt told me he actually had committed suicide by intentionally overdosing.

Now a single mother, Mom started working more, which left us at my aunt's house a lot. Eventually, Mom was able to purchase a mobile home with the insurance money Dad had left. When I was seven, Mom invited a man to live with us who eventually became my stepdad when they married. I was abused by him in every way possible—verbally, physically, sexually, and emotionally. It was torture for me.

The physical abuse mostly had to do with house cleaning. Our stepdad split the chores among my siblings and me. Sometimes, when I had to clean the bathroom, he would make me strip down naked and mix up ammonia and bleach in a bucket. As he left, he would lock the window and seal the door shut, leaving me to clean the bathroom with a toothbrush. Basically, if I came out before the room was spotless, I was in for a variety of abuse. This cleaning routine happened several times a month and for hours at a time. Also, he used to make me lick the toilet bowl clean.

Furthermore, he took great pleasure in forcing us to torture and kill our household pets. No animal was safe in our home. My stepdad would also slip into my room late at night and sexually abuse me. To protect myself, I was able to fall into a deep sleep while he was having sex with me. The sexual abuse continued for years. Later, when I went to therapy, my therapist explained to me his behaviors were the trademark of a psychopath.

I did not grow up in church, but I was always interested in and envious of people's church stories. I had heard about God and Jesus occasionally when my grandmother would take us to church services on Easter or Christmas. Since my stepdad was atheist, he didn't want us to believe in God. When I was twelve, I attended a Memorial Day service. The preacher's sermon was about how God can be your heavenly Father. He explained God sent His Son Jesus to die for us because He loves us so much and wants to adopt us into His family. Considering the father figures in my life so far, I was strongly drawn to having God as my Father. God was the Father I wanted.

With Holy Spirit conviction, I bolted down the aisle and dropped to my knees at the altar. I had 100 percent faith in Jesus and believed He had died for me. I begged God to be my dad. This was the day I got saved. I felt fully new and loved. This didn't mean that God would take everything bad away and my life would be perfect, no. Jesus even told the disciples their lives were going to be difficult at times. It's not easy being a Christian. After accepting Christ, I felt God's forgiveness toward my stepdad as if God had removed all my hate toward him. I even forgave my mom for not acknowledging what was going on with me and my stepdad. It didn't get easier; it actually got harder. The abuse got worse. When I got saved, God put on my heart a dream that He had for my life, and that was to be a missionary.

Now my stepdad had another reason to abuse me—I was a Christian. He wouldn't let me go to church. If he ever found a Christian CD, pamphlet, or Bible in my possession, he would destroy it in front of me or burn it. He would say, "If you are such a good Christian, you are supposed to obey your mother and father." After that, he would become very cruel and force me to do things against my will. My church at the time was in walking distance of my school, so I could lie and go to church. He caught on to me many times, and I paid for it through more abuse. Once I could drive, he would check the miles in my car because he knew the mileage to my school or work.

When I accepted Christ, I believed in Him fully. I would even pray before I ate a piece of candy. I would also pray for my stepdad while he was sexually abusing me. Earlier, I heard a song at church called "All My Praise" by Selah. God gave me the ability to memorize the song, and I would sing it over and over to myself while my stepfather was molesting me. That song got me through so much pain and sorrow. Yet there is only so much that praying and singing can do. I had God in my heart but didn't have His Word to read.

There were many kids in the home because not only did my mom and stepdad have their own daughter, but they also had adopted some kids. I was the only female being sexually abused in the home. The boys, however, were abused as well. This type of evil environment causes so much division between the siblings. Though I never wanted to see my siblings abused, there was a sense of relief when my stepdad's sights weren't set on me. My siblings and I were being tortured.

Once at church, I bravely opened up to a couple who were involved with the youth group. I told them what was going on at home, hoping they would do something about it. Their response to me was, "You must be doing really good things for God if the devil is trying so hard to get at you." That was all they said and all they did. Now that I am older, I can see there is some truth in that statement. But at that time, I was a minor in desperate need of help. That was a turning point for me in my spiritual walk. I thought if this was what it was like to be a Christian, I couldn't be one anymore. So I walked away from God.

After that, I was sharing a room with a girl cousin of mine who was later adopted into the family. I had just gotten out of the shower and gone into my bedroom where my cousin was. I shut the door. As I was changing behind the bed, my stepdad opened the door and started yelling about the door being shut. My cousin, still in the room, witnessed the whole situation. She heard him cursing and yelling at me, calling me worthless and pathetic because I had shut the door. He kept saying, "How many times do I have to tell you not to shut the door?" Finally, someone had witnessed what was going on.

After that, I told my mom what had happened, and she kicked him out. He was gone for the summer between my junior and senior year. When this happened, I mistakenly thought my mom was standing up for me and believed what I said he had done to me. However, I was sadly mistaken. Years later, to my surprise, I found out she actually kicked him out because he made a comment to my brother about being like his biological father.

I thought the summer was going to be great. I was going to be comfortable in my own house. Not long after my stepdad left, my mom felt guilty and sought the rest of the kids' permission to allow him back. Her reason was she didn't want their baby girl to grow up without a father. The majority of the children agreed, but I threatened to leave if he came back. It was an empty threat because I was sixteen with no place to go. Naturally, she spoke immediately to my stepdad. He moved back home. One evening when everyone in the house was gone except me and my stepdad, I paid dearly for telling my mom about the situation with my stepdad while my cousin was in the room. For about six or seven hours, I suffered the worse physical and sexual abuse ever. When my brothers were pulling up from football practice, my stepdad glanced out the window to see them, giving me a chance to throw on some clothes and bolt out the door. Vowing never to return, I got in my car and took off.

The last year of high school, I bounced from friend's house to friend's house. I would ask permission to stay the night and would stay for two weeks until I overstayed my welcome. I did this throughout my senior year until I graduated high school. After I graduated, though, my relationship with God was not good. During the following years, I didn't do anything wild or rebellious. Looking back, I can see that was because of the grace of God. I've seen so many people go through the same experiences as I did end up in a ditch somewhere with track marks or drunk. Some even turned to prostitution. I might have been just like them if it weren't for Jesus and His saving grace. Though I was not with God, God was with me.

I moved to another city after high school and became very

independent. On the anniversary of my dad's passing, I posted something on MySpace about being sad. Surprisingly, I received a message from a friend's older brother who was in the military. We chatted online for a month. When he received a new assignment, he came to Alabama to see his family. We spent a week together, and, at the end of the week, I moved with him to his new station in another state. We lived together for a year and nine months before we married. He seemed like a good guy and a Christian. Looking back, I see where there were signs and red flags that he was abusive. Compared to my stepdad, however, he was a saint.

To me, he seemed pretty wonderful. It was only after we married that the abuse really escalated. His abuse centered around my intellect. He would call me awful names, and it seemed everything I did was wrong. He was very controlling and jealous. He would hardly go to stores with me because I embarrassed him. He wouldn't go through a drive-through with me because I would want extra pickles, and that embarrassed him. He would make me walk in a single-file line if we went anywhere together, yanking my hand to get behind him or squeezing my hand if I got out of line. He once gave me a two-hour lecture on how to blow my nose properly because I was too dumb even to do that right.

Because of my earlier experiences, it never registered with me that this was abuse. The friends I met during this time were Christians, but we weren't actively seeking God and His Word. These people were a gift from God, and I am extremely close to them now. Though I didn't acknowledge God, my friends helped me realize my life was not okay.

He was gone a lot with the military during the two years we had been married. It was during this time my mom started having tingling and numbness in her legs. After testing, she was diagnosed with a tumor. My husband and I were able to make the eight-hour trip to Florida where my mom was having surgery to remove the growth. Following the surgery, the doctors told us they feared the tumor was cancerous, and they biopsied it. The diagnosis was melanoma. They told us that she had two weeks to two months to live because once the melanoma reached the spinal cord, she would be in stage four, which is terminal.

I went to a hotel that night and prayed desperately. Though I hadn't been praying much and didn't have an intimate relationship with God, I had faith in Him. I prayed that they would not find additional cancer or tumors in her body. The next day, they did the full-body scan and failed to find any other spots. Praise God! He was listening to me. Though her scan failed to disclose any other tumors, the original area of concern was a type of cancer that was super rare.

Melanoma is a skin cancer. It usually starts on your skin, but hers didn't. They cut off every suspicious freckle and mole. They scanned her entire body over and over again looking for other cancer sites, but none were found. Her type of cancer had a long and hard-to-pronounce name and was super, super rare. She was the first person in the US to have that type of cancer and the third person in the world. Because the cancer was so rare, they didn't know how to treat it. They did radiation and chemo. Surprising her doctors, she lived almost six years after her initial diagnosis. Either way, at that point we didn't know how long she had to live.

I always wanted Mom to meet her grandchild, so I asked her if she wanted me to have a baby. Knowing that I wasn't ready to be a mother and that she had always wanted me to go to college, she encouraged me to go to school. I was married to a military man, and I had a GI Bill enabling me to go anywhere I wanted. Everything would be paid. I started praying about where I wanted to go to college. Slowly but surely, God was pulling me back into an intimate relationship with Him through Mom's sickness. My husband wanted me to become a nurse or lawyer so I could make money wherever we moved. I didn't want those things, though.

I sat down with my paternal grandma, my favorite person on the planet, to discuss what I really wanted to do. My goal was to go to college and make sure Mom saw me graduate. My grandma started telling me she had retired from a restaurant as a waitress. She told me she absolutely loved her work. She loved her customers and memorizing their orders, so I hoped to do something that involved different crafts that I liked. I asked God to show me a sign. An advertisement for an art institute that was only two hours away from home flashed on the TV screen. It dawned on me that I should go to culinary school to become a cake decorator because it involved all the crafts I loved. I was able to register and enroll in culinary school.

In culinary school, I made two close friends who were my study buddies. We supported each other and did everything together. Going to school full time, I maintained a straight-A average. I discovered I was not the failure my husband accused me of being. It bolstered my confidence.

My four-hour drive to and from school was often quite exhausting. Fortunately, an old lady in our class, Ms. Mari, invited my friends and me to stay at her home if we didn't want to make the long drive home. For me it was a Godsend. She treated us like her own family. She even hosted my baby shower as well as my birthday party. She gave a party for my college classmates at her house. Since we were in culinary school, it wasn't a typical keg party: we had good food, wine, and cigars. About twenty students attended the party, including my two study buddies. We accepted an invitation to spend the night, and I thankfully climbed in bed and went to sleep. Because of my trauma from my childhood and teenage years, I could sleep through anything.

Sometime during the night or early morning, my study buddy

slipped into my room, and I woke up to find him raping me. When I yelled, he got off of me and ran out the door. He dropped out of school, and I never saw him again. Like most rape victims, I felt shame and told no one. I bottled it all up, putting a smile on my face, pretending that everything was okay, just as I had done for years. Six weeks later, I discovered I was pregnant. I had no clue if I had gotten pregnant by my husband or the guy who raped me. I didn't want to know. When I told my husband I was pregnant, he was not happy. He refused to go to the ultrasounds and refused to hear the baby's heartbeat. He didn't want anything to do with the whole process. It was a very lonely pregnancy for me. However, my mom's goals were fulfilled: I graduated college and had a baby boy.

I didn't realize everyone in the military had to go to Korea for a year until my husband told me that he was to leave. I was relieved. I was in a survivalist mindset and looked forward to a whole year of no abuse. I was also unaware that the military had a provision that if you or your spouse had a family member with a terminal illness, the military would terminate your deployment and station you closer to your family so you could take care of them. Secretly, my husband and mom worked out a plan: she would go to the doctor and receive false documentation indicating her illness was terminal. I was unaware of this and was totally surprised when he came back from Korea a month later.

During the time he was gone for the month, my baby was six months old. I failed to clean my house. I developed anxiety about cleaning and had panic attacks every time I tried to clean. Looking at the mess, I couldn't breathe. I saw a therapist. A friend, who was neat and obsessed with cleanliness, had the same therapist. The therapist suggested we could both benefit by cleaning my house together. I did all the exercises the therapist recommended. Working with my friend, I learned how to keep my house clean and maintain it.

I had many sessions with my therapist. I was able to tell my therapist about my childhood abuse. She gave me several exercises to help me open up. One exercise had me write a letter to the key people in my childhood. I then read it aloud to an empty chair, pretending the key person was sitting there listening. Afterward I could keep the letter, burn it, tear it up, or give it to the therapist. Through this exercise, my therapist learned all about both my childhood and spousal abuses.

After I attended the sessions for several months, the therapist encouraged me to cry. I had never been able to cry, holding in all my agony. I was puzzled about my inability to cry and asked the therapist what she thought. She encouraged me to figure it out, but I never could. She told me the following: "All the years your stepdad tortured you, you were a victim, just a little girl. Though you were helpless, there was one thing you could do, and that was your power to withhold tears." It was a sign of strength and survival, but now it was okay to release those tears.

My mom and sister made a trip to visit me the month my husband was in Korea. My mom noticed I was making positive changes, and she was proud of my clean house. During the visit, I noticed my sister exhibiting behaviors that concerned me. She would never laugh at herself and would hit herself, calling herself pathetic and worthless—the very words my stepdad used to call me. She was exhibiting signs of abuse.

I knew God was tugging on my heartstrings, but I could not tell Mom the truth. One afternoon we were sitting outside on the patio, and Mom got a call from my stepdad. She was talking to the man who abused me, and I lost my cool. I told her to get off the phone, and she did. Angry, I blurted out a sentence I had practiced with the therapist, saying, "(Insert my stepdad's name) did things to me, so you need to protect my baby sister." Mom was totally confused and asked me what had happened.

I encouraged her to sit down with my therapist and me, and I would reveal everything.

Over the course of several days, Mom could not make up her mind whether she wanted to know what had happened or not. I needed my mom to know everything and stand up for me. Finally, she agreed to go, and I made the appointment. Shortly before we were to meet with the therapist, mom told me she couldn't go, and she didn't. I attended the meeting and explained what had happened. The therapist encouraged me to share my feelings with Mom and ask her to take action and protect my sister. Finally, my mom agreed to go to therapy with me. At that meeting I told my mom everything. I shared all the graphic details about the abuse. During this meeting was the second time I shared my story in full. The first time I blacked out, so I was thankful for only having a panic attack this time. Mom's reaction was anger. All of a sudden, she started crying and said, "I never wanted you to have my life." My poor mom had been abused by her stepdad too. We talked about Mom's childhood with the therapist. I was able to give Mom details about my abuse, enabling her to confront my stepdad. That confrontation didn't happen all at once. I had to have a lot of grace and patience, but she eventually confronted my stepdad, and they got a divorce.

When my husband returned from Korea, the abuse didn't stop. We moved to Florida, and I tried everything to save the marriage. I tried therapy. I encouraged him to go to church. I tried praying and reading my Bible. I tried everything I could. Now my husband began physically abusing both me and my son. All it took was one time, and I had to leave. Ultimately, I got a divorce.

My mom left my stepdad, and I left my husband. God used everything I had experienced and worked it out for our good in my family of women. He brought an end to abusive marriages through which women, children, or both were deeply hurt. God used my rape and pregnancy to work a miracle. Every single thing I have been through is related to Romans 8:28 (KJV): "And we know that all things work together for good to them that love God, to them who are the called according to his purpose." I know my God is powerful.

My son and I moved back to Alabama to live with my mom and baby sister for a couple of months. It was not an easy time. Though Mom had been in remission for years, her cancer had returned, and she was in a lot of pain. She was unable to move around much anymore and spent a great deal of time resting. Though she was going through a divorce, she missed my stepdad and tried to date him again. She added stress to my life by trying to encourage me to get back with my husband. She would post sticky notes about love being patient and kind throughout the house. Unfortunately, because of this, we would fight a lot.

Mom was mad at me for telling the truth about my stepdad, but I had to tell her to protect my sister, a vulnerable thirteen-year-old. At this time my relationship with God was not strong. My prayer life was erratic. I just kept praying, "Thy will be done in every situation," but I never went to Him about the specifics. I was so far away from God, but He was near to me. During my entire pregnancy, I had prayed above all else that God's will would be done.

Out of the blue, one of my mom's coworkers invited her to a nearby church, and Mom encouraged me to go with her. At this point I was at rock bottom. I was having nightmares every night. I was raising a baby but didn't know which man was the father. I was grieving my mom's suffering. When she encouraged me to go to church, I longed to go.

We attended the evening service at the church, and the title of the message was "God's Will." It's incredible how God is in the details all the time. I had been praying for God's will for years.

The message spoke to me. I kept coming back to this church, and every message after that kept speaking to me. Slowly but surely, I was returning to God. I was trusting God with my life. During my prayer one night, I said the following to God: "I left You, but You never left me. I can see You have been with me through all of this, but I have made a mess of everything. My life is a mess right now. This is what happens when I am in control, and now I want to surrender completely." God answered my prayers. Though my husband told me for years that I would never survive without him and that I could never take care of myself, I proved him wrong. I was about to get my own place and a job. It was empowering to be on my own and know that with God's help I could be a successful single mom.

Sometimes it's difficult to figure out our purposes in life. Like many people, I couldn't make up my mind about which path to take. I chose to go to Bible college, and that's when God reminded me of my purpose and His dream for my life, which was to be a missionary. I would like to say getting back in church and furthering my relationship with God was an overnight thing, but it wasn't.

As I was mending my relationship with God, I connected with a friend from the past. Tessa had a little girl the same age as my son, and we spent time together. Unfortunately, my friend was an atheist who partied and drank a lot. I would tag along with her, and occasionally I would drink a beer. Sometimes, though, I felt convicted about it. I was not the best example of a Christian for her. I invited her to church one day, and she attended, but she chose not to go back.

Due to domestic problems, she vowed to leave her husband though I tried to talk her out of it. Though the divorce proceedings were ongoing and not yet finished, she dated a coworker of mine. Tessa's ex-husband had custody of their daughter throughout the week, and Tessa had her on the weekends. One night Tessa banged on his door and demanded to have their daughter, but he refused to hand her over because Tessa seemed disoriented. I knew nothing about this until her boyfriend called me and said he was going to check on her because something was not right. Her boyfriend arrived at her home and found her unresponsive on the couch. She started violently seizing, and when the paramedics arrived, she began seizing again. At the hospital, when they pumped her stomach, they found it full of blue liquid. The doctors feared she had drunk some Windex or other cleaning products. I called her sister-in-law, who passed on the information to the rest of the family. Tessa was flown to another hospital because she was so gravely ill.

While the medics prepared her for the flight, the police asked me to go with them to her apartment. They searched through all her belongings and her trash, where they found beer cans and liquor bottles. While I was watching the policemen sift through everything, an officer opened one of her college books and found a suicide note addressed to her daughter. I was deeply shocked and depressed, but I was able to leave my son and stay with Tessa at the nearby hospital.

Because the divorce wasn't final, her husband was in charge of her care. Therefore, her boyfriend was asked to leave. Her in-laws remained at the hospital to support and comfort their son. When it became clear that Tessa would not survive because her organs were shutting down, the doctors suggested she be taken off life support. Shortly after this, her ex's family and some of her family members entered the room as the priest prayed for her. There was a commotion in the hall, and we heard someone running to the door. Apparently, Tessa's license indicated she was an organ donor, so someone was asking permission to harvest her organs. The donation would take eighteen hours, both to complete the paperwork and find recipients.

Her husband agreed to the donation and requested time for the family members to say their goodbyes. I had been asked to text her boyfriend when she had passed, but I was unable to inform him about the new developments. When the family members had a chance to be with Tessa, I was able to go into the room. It was then the Holy Spirit convicted me to share the Gospel with her. In my testimony, I talked about when Jesus saved me at the age of twelve and that I had not been living a good Christian life. Wanting to see her in heaven one day, I encouraged her to pray and believe in God, and if she did that wholeheartedly, she would wake up in heaven. I poured out my heart and reminded her of what Jesus had done for her. Suddenly, my phone rang, and her boyfriend was on the line. I put the phone up to her ear and let him say his goodbyes. I explained I had been trying to reach him all day and that it was a miracle that he had called when I was alone in the room with her.

Following his call, I talked to Tessa for twenty more minutes. I explained how real God is and that He was trying to reach out to her. Additionally, I reassured her that I would look after her daughter, and, closing my eyes, I said a prayer. I took her through the Romans Road and explained how she could be saved. When I opened my eyes, she was crying. Her tears were significant because there had been no movement from her in days. I fully believe that when I get to heaven, she will be there. My time with Tessa is proof that God is willing to use ordinary people in extraordinary ways.

I was overwhelmed by Tessa's death; I knew I couldn't lose another friend or family member. It was at this moment I realized I had to share what God had done for me. I knew I had to reach out to people and let them know God can be their Father, too, and He would adopt them into His great family. This was the moment my life completely changed. I started earnestly pursuing God more.

I realized God had taken each and every thing I had been through and used it to bless people in ways I could never imagine.

Our church planned yearly mission trips to various countries. About a month after my friend died, our church planned a new overseas trip. Wondering if I should go on the mission, I asked God for His guidance. One of our preachers asked if I was going on the trip, and when I hesitated to answer, he told me I was going. To prove God's answer, He provided a babysitter for my son.

I went on the best trip ever to the Dominican Republic. The people there live in abject poverty. In this culture, the men control the families. Their wives and children suffer abuse similar to my experiences. I had to find a way to effectively reach these people who desperately needed Jesus. My camera and high school Spanish became the way I could share the Gospel. I wasn't just some white girl from America who had grown up in a perfect home. I was a girl who could deeply relate to these people. Because of this, people could open up and say, "Me too." Those words are two of the most powerful words in ministry. I could look at these people and say, "Me too, I've been there. I know what you are going through. Let me tell you what God did for me. Let me tell you how He helped me out."

If you had a dad who committed suicide,
I could talk to you about that.
If you went through abuse as a child,
I could talk to you about that.
If you were raped and conceived a child
and had to raise it on your own,
I could talk to you about that.
If you had a parent who had cancer,
I could talk to you about that.
If you had a friend who committed suicide,
I could talk to you about that.

During this mission, I witnessed to children for the first time. I was partnered with a translator who helped me share the Gospel with a twelve-year-old boy who went with us the next day to invite people to watch a movie about Jesus. To our surprise, the boy and his friend had already invited everyone to church; he had done our work for us! The translator and I thought a reward was in order. The mission's pastor suggested that both the translator and I go to a tiny ice cream shop to buy the boys some ice cream. My concern, however, was that women with blonde hair and blue eyes were considered angels, and I fit that description. Children would look up to these women, yet men would kidnap and gang-rape them. I was fearful but remembered the leader saying God's authority would protect us. As we walked down to the ice cream shop, a group of little children surrounded us. They had no idea we were surprising them with ice cream. The lady who owned the shop had gotten saved the day before and was excited to see us. We told the twelve-year-old boy that we were proud that he had just gotten saved and he was already inviting people to the Jesus movie and sharing the Gospel with others. We told them we were giving them all ice cream as a thank-you gift.

The children were thrilled about the ice cream. The translator and I were sitting in the store as the delighted children received and ate their ice cream as a quick afternoon storm started. The Holy Spirit prompted me to share the Gospel with the children. I've never done that before and feared I couldn't explain it in a way they could understand. I trusted the Holy Spirit to speak through me and accepted His request. After I told the translator my plans, he questioned me, but I remained firm. The rain immediately stopped, prompting the children to leave to go watch the movie.

Following the Holy Spirit's instructions, I called the children back inside and began to share the Gospel with them all. The Holy

Spirit then spoke through me, holding the children's interest. I asked if they were saved, and they were not, with the exception of the young boy who invited people to the Jesus movie. I used the ice cream as an example to explain the gift of Jesus. With the Holy Spirit's words, I told them that they could pray and accept Jesus, and that I would lead them through a prayer. They could choose to make a decision, but only if they were serious. With the translator's help, I bowed my head and started praying. Then I heard a chorus of children say the prayer after me.

When I finished and looked up, I was shocked: we had come into the ice cream shop with only five kids; now there were fourteen kids surrounding us that had accepted Christ in that moment. The whole trip was just encounter after encounter like that. My lesson from the trip was this truth: Anytime God tells you to go somewhere, you go. It will be worth it every time. Regardless of where you are, God will open the door, enabling you to relate to people on a personal level.

In a span of two years, I had accepted the call to be a missionary as well as to start a ministry. This undertaking was not easy, and many times I was vulnerable to the attacks of Satan, which caused me to stumble. It was only after I was actually sharing my story with someone that I realized this was the same way I drifted away from God when my earlier life was miserable. However, now, I was grounded in God's Word. I had a weapon, a tool, the armor to use against Satan: the Bible.

During these two years, twelve family members and close friends passed away. The grief I felt left me depressed for a few months. Suddenly, when I was sharing my story with someone, God revealed to me it was Satan making my life miserable, just as he did before. Using God's truth as well as His comfort and love, I was able to go back and help others.

During this time several amazing works of God occurred. Out of the blue, my ex-husband decided he wanted full custody of our son, but later he changed his mind. His decision changed almost every week, causing me great emotional distress. Our court battle seemed never ending.

At this time I was working full time. I felt God was telling me to drop to part-time work, which made no sense. I feared dropping to part time in the middle of a custody battle would be viewed negatively. The managers put pressure on me to start working Sundays. That was when I knew I had to let go of control and be obedient to God and work part time. I sat down with my manager and explained that I didn't want to work on Sundays because it was the day of the Lord. My manager graciously allowed me to work part time. Working part time enabled me to spend time with my dying mom. It was during one of these visits that my aunt, my father's sister, sat quietly with me by my mom's hospital bed, which had been placed in the living room. As we sat together, my mom passed away.

Concerned with my aunt's lack of salvation, I turned to my aunt and felt the Holy Spirit lead me to share the Gospel with her. I asked my aunt to come with me into another room, but at that moment, a group of relatives and friends walked in. Despite the interruption, my aunt and I were able to leave the living room and speak together. My aunt was an atheist and strong in her belief, but God used my testimony and Mom's death as instruments to enable my aunt to accept Christ after my mom passed away. This was the first amazing work of God.

Later, when going through my mom's things, I checked her phone and discovered that on an app called Prayers, my mom had listed my aunt's name on a prayer for salvation. My sweet mom had done this a year and a half prior to her death. I opened it up and read, "Praying for (insert aunt's name) salvation no matter how it has to happen." I just know my mom was in heaven rejoicing with the angels over a soul saved. The second amazing work of God occurred months later when my ex-husband dropped his custody suit. After months of praying, my heart was lifted by God's great gift, and I never had to worry about losing my son again.

I have seen God do so many things like this in my life, and I am beyond grateful. I would willingly go through the torture and torment that I've experienced just to see one more minute of God's glory at work. It is my joy to see His will be done and completely changing a situation and turning it into something amazing and good for His glory, as well as for the furtherance of His kingdom. To see a soul set free and one day heaven bound is the reason I am perfectly happy sharing the Gospel every day until the day I die and wake up on the other side with Jesus. Words cannot express that feeling of sharing the Gospel with someone and witnessing them go from spiritual death to eternal life through Jesus Christ, knowing they will never be alone because God is their Father. No matter what they go through, life will work out if they just trust Him.

Earlier, during tough times, I spent a weekend fasting and reading God's Word. I decided to take out a piece of paper and make two columns. The first column listed all the evil I had experienced; the second column listed the blessings I had received. After comparing the two, the blessings on the right side were more powerful and awesome than the circumstances on the left side. I learned this truth: God will work in mighty ways through unbelievable circumstances for those that love Him and through this, bring Him glory. Your part requires surrender and sacrifice. If you persevere though the pain, your relationship with Christ will deepen. God can use me and you. Where sin abounds, grace will flourish. There is a beginning and end to every story. I am living in the middle, but I can't wait until the end.

WONDERFUL

Wonderful ▪

This is a man's story of violence, drugs, and alcohol. A marriage begins in a drug dealer's house. They hit rock bottom, yet they serve a wonderful Savior named Jesus Christ. Sit with me now as we walk in the shoes of a young man who turns to all the evil life has to offer while losing himself. He finds mercy and grace in the love of a wonderful Father.

What I can remember of my life as a child is not good. We did not have a normal family environment. In our home there were constant fights, guns, and violence. My dad was a heavy drinker, which brought out the worst in him. There were times that the fighting escalated to the point of weapons being pulled and glass broken. The final straw for my mom occurred when my dad held her hostage at gunpoint for three days. The following day, as he left for work, she picked me up from school, and we moved to Montana to live with my uncle.

When I was thirteen years old, I started to experiment with drugs and alcohol. When I was fifteen, my mom received a call from the police informing her that while driving and drinking, my father had killed himself and a young expectant couple. I remember "I hate you" were the last words I said to my dad. After my dad passed away, drinking and using drugs with my friends were normal activities for me.

I graduated from high school and started to attend a small

junior college, but I quickly found out college was not for me. I lived with my best friend and his dad at the time, but I left them to hang out with a different crowd. I was running from the truth, reality, hurt, and pain. At the age of twenty, I flunked college due to my crystal meth addiction. Shortly after, I received two DUIs in two different states in less than two weeks. I bounced from place to place, never thinking about those around me. I tried to get clean on my own. I went to Mom's house, where she allowed me to detox. After about two weeks of misery, I was sober. I was thinking somewhat clearly and decided I was going to do better. However, my problems followed me, and in a short while, I was addicted again.

Around the age of twenty-six, I moved to Alabama to live with my sister, and hid my addiction from everyone. There I met a woman who had two teenage daughters. Following our initial meeting at our drug dealer's house, we began to hang out and do drugs together. Within a short time, we were married and struggling. We had to work to support our habits, and though we had found a house to rent, it became extremely difficult to pay all of our bills and support our addictions. To bring in more money, I decided to manufacture meth.

My wife and I lost everything we had. We were homeless, living in a Chevy Tahoe. We had no friends or family who wanted us near them. We hit rock bottom. My mother-in-law invited us to live in her home and attend her church. Though we resisted at first, we finally moved in with her and went to church in August 2010. Church wasn't as bad as I expected, and I did not get struck by lightning! My wife and I decided to go back the next Sunday. During the service, I surrendered my life to Christ, and it was the greatest day of my life. From that day forth, my life has been transformed.

It has by no means been an easy path to follow Jesus Christ. Soon after I surrendered my life to Christ and joined the church, we became involved in serving in the church, and things seemed to be looking up. One day after church, we left to go help with a Relay for Life event. On our way home from Relay for Life, the police pulled us over. I knew at that time I had a warrant for a traffic violation. The police informed us that my wife had one as well. Needless to say, we both were arrested and went to jail.

At first the situation was devastating because we were excited about serving and helping in church. In reflection, however, I knew this needed to happen. To be right with God, I needed to be cleared of any offense to the law. We arrived at the jail, got booked in, and discovered it would be a few days before we could see the judge, so we would be in jail a few days. We made our calls and entered holding cells to wait. About an hour or so into our incarceration, I turned to God. I surrendered. I began to pray these words: "Lord, as long as I am here, I'll either hear some preaching or do some preaching." At the moment I surrendered, I was free. It wasn't long until we were both released. I look back to that day now and understand that at that moment, right in that cell, I surrendered to preach. God, in His wisdom, called me to preach the Gospel and opened the door for me to go to Bible college.

God is wonderful! He has done so much for my wife and me, even though we do not deserve it. We have been married for eleven and a half years, blessed years. During this time, God has allowed me to go into the world to minister to others in need. I could have never dreamed of the true joy that God has given me in His Son Jesus Christ. I now have peace, provision, and power through the Holy Spirit. God will take what is broken or marred and make something beautiful: His image in me and in you if you will allow Him.

MERCIFUL

Merciful ▪

"Enjoyable" and "carefree" describe her childhood. One of those unforgettable nights in college leads to her life being changed forever. She feels unworthy and uncomfortable in her own skin but finds restoration in a merciful Father.

Growing up, I was always the responsible one, the rule follower. I was both respectful and well behaved. My childhood was wonderful and carefree. I was very involved in church, made a profession of faith at the age of six, and could tell you several Bible stories. I had always done the right thing, or rather, I played the role, I guess you could say.

Then, senior year, high school graduation, and freshman year in college arrived. Moving away from home, being independent, and exploring the freedoms all that brought changed me. I found myself partying, drinking, and living "the college life." My life was great, or so I thought.

One of those unforgettable nights I spent partying changed my life forever. I was sexually abused. Through my carelessness and disobedience, I placed myself in a harmful and dangerous situation that led to a traumatic event, causing my life to spiral out of control.

I began to fail my classes, and I developed severe anxiety as well as an extreme hatred for myself. I believed that I deserved the abuse due to my actions. Several months later, I discovered that I was pregnant. This just intensified my anxiety and shame.

I finally told my parents about my situation. Initially I feared they would reject me, but they laid my fears to rest by being very supportive. At the age of nineteen, I became a mother to my precious son. I was just another teen mom statistic, trying to raise my son. That is how I viewed my life for several years. Because of my family's support, I was able to continue and complete my academic goals and receive a degree.

My life was in shambles as I tried to control everything in my life. I was working, attending college, raising a child, and living with my parents. I felt the need for complete independence but knew staying with my parents was best. I was finished with myself, even contemplating suicide in the darkest times, and I was convinced God was finished with me too. The only thing that kept me going was my son. No matter what church I attended, how good I tried to be, nothing changed. I had to be stronger than I felt. I prayed and begged God to help me. At my lowest, God strengthened me.

During this time, I was diagnosed with obsessive-compulsive disorder as a result of the sexual trauma. Life was hard. At times I did not think I would survive. I was overwhelmed, wounded, and ready to give up. There were times I could not stand to be in my own skin. I talked with a mentor who helped me compartmentalize my emotions and need for control when my world seemed to spin endlessly. However, I continued to seek God, raise my child in church, and try to be the best mom I knew how to be.

At my lowest point, a friend invited me to visit her church. At the church I had been attending, I felt the congregation was judgmental toward me. After several invites from another friend, I finally agreed to attend her church. At this church, the congregation accepted me and showed me a Christ-like love. Here I experienced hope. Then, one glorious day, I truly accepted Christ's gift of love and eternal salvation. My life was once again changed, and I was restored completely.

I knew I had disappointed God in the past, but oh how merciful He is! He did not allow me to wallow in my self-pity. He cleaned me up and gave me a new life, including a wonderful husband, five beautiful children, and an adorable grandchild. God certainly had every right to be finished with me. However, He is compassionate, forgiving, and tolerant. He is *merciful!* He loved me when I could not love myself. He sought me when I did not want to be found. When I felt dirty, He made me clean. When I wanted to give up, He was just getting started.

I still struggle with feeling dirty and unworthy; however, all I have to do is think of God's grace and mercy and remind myself that I am a child of God with full benefits. Compassionate, gracious, forgiving, tolerant: these are all words used to define the word *merciful.* They are also the words that I use to describe my God.

REDEEMED

Redeemed ∎

In the stronghold of pornography, he is living a lie while playing the part of the perfect Christian. Though broken and struggling with addiction, with his wife standing faithfully by his side, he finds redemption through Jesus Christ.

Growing up, I had a nurturing home life. I had great parents, a wonderful family, and more than I needed. My dad was a pastor and a well-known politician. Living in a small town, I always had to be on my best behavior, making sure I didn't reflect negatively on the family. To this day, I remember when we got a computer with Windows 95 and dial-up internet. When I was thirteen, the internet had become faster and had many more options. My friends told me I could find anything online, and I began surfing the web.

From that moment forward when I was alone, at least once a week, I was looking up whatever I could think of. I didn't really care if my parents caught me. It was at this time I discovered pornography. When I was old enough to stay home by myself, I would sit for hours looking through various websites. When I turned sixteen, my smartphone allowed me to indulge in my passion, anytime, anywhere. For the next ten years, I escaped into the world of pornography. It was a secret no one had to know but me.

During this time, I was still going to church every Sunday, singing in Gospel groups, and demonstrating I was the world's best Christian, even though I was the world's worst hypocrite. Soon, watching porn was not good enough, so I started talking to women I met on the internet. Though I was able to keep a working schedule and a job, I often locked myself in the house, settling down to talk to women and watch porn.

At this point in my addiction, I thought meeting a woman was the answer to all of my problems. Shortly thereafter I met a woman who was wonderful and merciful. *This woman might be the answer I'm seeking*, I thought. I hid my addiction from her, and eventually, we married. Not long after our wedding I committed adultery and tried to hide that as well. Because she had access to my cell phone, she was able to find pictures and voicemails I had forgotten to delete. I felt my life was over. I feared my wife was going to leave me, exposing the kind of person I truly was.

However, God had given me a caring wife. She chose to stay with me and tried to save our marriage. Marriage counseling with a pastor friend helped us so much. During this time, we attended a night service at our church. Our pastor's sermon was on the story of Jacob, who lied and conned people for gain and ultimately, wrestled with God. I, too, was wrestling with God. When the pastor invited us to come to the altar, I answered the call and received the saving grace of Jesus.

Today, my wife and I are still married and have completed two years of counseling. We are expecting our first baby, a boy. My wife has been by my side on this journey, and I am thankful to God for blessing me with this amazing and forgiving woman. God has allowed me the opportunity to be an accountability partner with men struggling with my same addiction. I speak to teenagers about the dangers of pornography and what it can do to our minds.

The road to recovery has not been an easy one, and I have had my setbacks, but God loved me so much that He chastised me to walk His path. It has taken more than pastoral counseling to get where I am today. With the blessing of professionals at a treatment center that I spent almost two months in, and with the help of many recovery friends, I press on to a healthier life. I do pray that men have heavenly guarded eyes and minds since technology is an easy gateway into sin and destruction. Cry out to Jesus, and He will save you from the pornography and addiction that rip families apart. If Jesus saved a sinner like me, He can do the same for you.

There are so many people, both men and women, who struggle with pornography, and many people are afraid to get help. Don't be ashamed; there are resources to help. There are support groups, therapists who specialize in pornography, and literature. There is also support for the spouses because they, too, need support. There are amazing hope and freedom in recovery. All it takes is the first step of courage and faith to say, "I need help."

■ FORGIVING

Forgiving ∎

Growing up in a drug dealer's home, he knows no other reality outside of escaping into the world of drugs, pornography, and TV entertainment in attempts to numb the pain of loss in life. He looks for comfort in all the wrong places, only to find himself at the feet of a forgiving Father.

I had been taught about Jesus from the time I could sing songs (you know, "Jesus loves me, this I know, for the Bible tells me so"). Growing up, my mom worked, and I spent most days with my dad. He had bad anger issues, and he had never known what real love, God's agape love, was, so he couldn't share that love with me. For instance, I knew I had completed a task to my dad's standard only because he had not yelled or cursed at me during the process. That didn't happen often, if ever, but I didn't realize this wasn't normal until I met my heavenly Father. My mother and father were affectionate to me and my brother, but they didn't have the means to nurture us and provide for us the way we needed.

My dad used and sold drugs from our house, leaving us on our own most of the time. Normal home life looked like my parents having a bunch of friends over, all piled in their bedroom, trying to keep nosy kids out. I figured out they were using and selling drugs in there, even though they tried to keep me distracted. I even remember seeing them at the kitchen table snorting cocaine once. Even if there wasn't a bunch of people at the house, which didn't happen often, my brother and parents would still smoke marijuana at home. As a result, I often retreated into a fantasy world based on television programs, movies, comic books, and eventually pornography. My mom attended church sporadically for many years of my childhood; we would go to church with her very inconsistently, or with my grandmother.

When I was thirteen, my brother died at the age of twenty-three in an accident. He fell on a knife while he was making a sandwich. Holding the knife as he turned to walk away, he slipped, and while trying to brace himself, he fell on the blade. This tragedy destroyed everyone in our family, and I often found myself consoling my mom even though I had an empty heart. I did not understand how to process this grief, so I would escape into my false reality.

I hated God for taking my hero away, and the only defense I had against my dad. My brother was ten years older than me and was often my escape. When he sensed trouble between my parents, he took me outside or down to the barn, where we fed the horses until things settled down inside. Without him, I went into a very dark place of anger and hate. I found a place to escape my pain through drugs and adult magazines. I easily got caught up in looking at pornography.

At some point within the next year, I don't remember the occasion, but Mom and I attended a nearby church where I had been many times before. I don't remember the message, but I remember having this horrible thought: I would never see my brother again if I was not saved, even though I wasn't sure of his salvation. That day I went to the altar, and as I cried, the preacher prayed over me. When I got up, I felt better, but went back to living life the same as I always had.

My choices and the devil's trickery took me out of church for the better part of the next fifteen years of my life. I continued to use both porn and TV entertainment to avoid realities and numb emotions I didn't know how to process. I couldn't handle the death of friends or family members, social anxieties, rejection, anger, and the like. I got hooked on many drugs, from meth to Xanax, and sometimes both at the same time. Despite all of this, God in His faithfulness kept me from serious danger, kept me out of prison, and often used me as the voice of reason in my group of friends, keeping us from doing some terrible things.

I went back to church when a friend invited me. I had never felt so wanted or accepted in a church, ever. I had also never been to a church that put so much importance on discipleship, and that really got my attention. I continued to visit off and on for almost a year. Right before I started going to that church, I met a girl in the drug scene. We started casually hanging out and partying together, and eventually we had a child together. The girl, although she didn't want anything to do with me, allowed me to see my son. Eventually, I was compelled to invite her to come with me to church, and we started going together and growing in Christ, getting discipled. As we continued to seek God, our lives became more disciplined. We felt convicted our lifestyle had to change with God's guidance. We were married, and, shortly thereafter, my wife got saved.

For years, I thought that the day I prayed at the altar after my brother died was the day I got saved, even though every so often while struggling with temptation and sin, I would cry out to God and ask Him, "If I am not saved, please save me." I thought I was saved because I "felt" God. Then one day someone shared a message with me that changed my life. That man took a Bible and showed me evidence of salvation that I did not have in my life. He used the Bible to teach me the difference between worldly sorrow and Godly sorrow. At that moment God opened my eyes and helped me see that I was, in fact, a sinner, and that my sin had offended a holy and perfect God. I acknowledged my sin to Him and asked Him to forgive and save me. In that moment, I finally felt the wholeness and peace that I had heard people talk about. It wasn't based on the "God bumps," but on God's Word.

Since that day, things have been different. God has helped me to face sins and addictions I kept hidden and ran from for years. He has given me a desire to spend time with Him in His Word, and with the Holy Spirit, He has given me the ability to be the kind of husband and father I have wanted to be but couldn't be on my own. I finally understand and have the unconditional love that I have searched for my entire life. I am overwhelmed by the ways He protected me even though I was lost. He had a plan for me, and I am so grateful that I get to live it.

God is faithful to use my mistakes for good, and He never gave up on me, even though I disobeyed Him many times by using pornography. Through therapy and His loving guidance, I am now on a path to recovering and retraining my brain. He is using my brokenness to heal me.

God has blessed me with my wife and four amazing children. God has allowed me to see my wife, my father, and my three oldest children all get saved. God has blessed me with a great home and stability in my life. God has given me an awesome church family who are often more like family than my actual family. He has pointed me in the direction of a great ministry where God's story in me has made a difference in people's lives, people who are hurting and broken, just like me. I know He is always with me. Even in my disobedience, even in my drug use, He was always with me. In my lowest of lows and my highest of highs, He has always been there. I always give Him the glory.

STEADFAST

Steadfast ∎

Feeling like an outsider everywhere she goes, she tries to earn the attention and approval of others. She finds escape through drugs and men. While she longs to be loved and accepted, she finds her identity in a heavenly Father who is steadfast.

I was born in northern Alabama, second in a family that eventually had three sons and one daughter. Having already experienced some of the difficulties that life can offer, my parents were married a few months before I was conceived. With no sisters of my own, my playmates of choice were limited to my younger brothers or my girl cousins, when visits could be arranged. My oldest brother from my mother's first marriage did not want anything to do with me. In fact, he seemed to adopt as his life's mission making me miserable, or at the very least, feeling bothersome and unimportant.

My father worked tirelessly at a cabinet shop and would come home smelling of sawdust and paint. As a result of this family of six living solely off my father's income, there was never room in the budget for many extracurricular activities and other extras. I remember wearing my older brother's hand-me-downs to school, for example. That said, it wasn't until later in life that I realized our family might have been considered poor; I just thought my parents were mean. However, my brothers and I never lacked basic necessities. We always celebrated happy Christmases and birthdays, and I remember going on several family vacations or extended family reunion-type trips, although most of those were camping affairs. Wonderful memories, nonetheless. But we never had extras.

My dad took a job at a cabinet company in a town south of Huntsville, Alabama, when I was six. He commuted at first, but eventually my parents moved us to be closer to his work. In that transition, I lost all my friends at school and my very best friend, a girl cousin who was only six months younger than me. The school we started attending wasn't terrible, but I was an outsider and would never fully overcome that. It was hard making friends. At home, my brothers would gang up on me and pick fights or steal my stuff or just completely isolate me. They called me names and threw insults at me. At this time, Mom was in college trying to earn her degree in psychology. With both of my parents out of the house, I had no reprieve from that particular line of attack. If ever I turned to my parents for help, I would get waved away, with some response along the lines of, "Not now," "I'm working," "Figure it out yourself," "Quit being so dramatic," "Life isn't fair," and the list goes on.

This pervasive sense of injustice slowly started creeping into my hurt little mind, and in time, I started getting labeled as bossy, or a tattletale, or a know-it-all. I found myself feeling like everyone considered me a nuisance, including my parents. I don't remember my mother defending my little broken, lonely heart during these years, but rather she added to my pain of emotional dysfunction and neglect. Mom was permanently frazzled and exhausted from caring for four children while going to night school full time. To make matters worse for her, my father was also a closet, functioning alcoholic, although I did not know it at the time. Eventually, my mom graduated and got a good job.

By that time, my brothers and I were old enough to mostly care for ourselves. Sibling rivalries, however, only intensified, oftentimes resulting in cursing or fistfights, and rarely were relational boundaries mended during these times. I will say, though, that the majority of the disputes were between me and either my oldest brother or the brother following me. My youngest brother was often the peacekeeper, and he was easier on me than the other two. Occasionally, he would even let me join his play or would accompany me in mine.

During these early years of childhood, my parents took us to church nearly every Sunday. My mother was raised in a staunch Catholic household, and my father in an equally strict Baptist household, so when they married, they "compromised" with the Episcopal church. We would fight over hair and clothes, cry over torn pantyhose or scuffed shoes, and then walk into church with tear-streaked cheeks and smiling faces, go to our Sunday school classes. There we would hear sweet Bible stories about Jesus or cute rhymes to help us remember the books of the Bible, and then we'd go home and not talk about Jesus again until the next Sunday. Oh sure, we prayed during the week: the same prayer over dinner every night, and, if reminded, the same memorized prayer at bedtime each night. Our parents would use a Bible verse at the table to remind us of our places. When at the dinner table one night, I asked if I could please have another roll, my mother eyed my untouched green beans and pork roast, sighed a deep sigh of exasperation, and said to me, "Man cannot live by bread alone."

But for the most part, my parents did not live out an example of Godly Christian life. They did have standards and morals for us children: there were certain things we could not watch on TV, we could not go to certain people's houses, and we had other restrictions of this sort. My parents, on the other hand, drank and cussed and smoked cigarettes and fought angrily and gossiped, all with an underlying holier-than-that-neighbor-across-the-street attitude.

My mother, when angry, would use such demeaning language and tone of voice that I could feel myself shrink. And, of course, this did nothing to console the hurt and lonely little girl inside me, whom I could feel crying out louder every day, "Love me! Accept me! Spend time with me! Like me!" My mother had a distinct way of letting you know that your good efforts were not meeting her standard. She was very good at nitpicking and micromanaging everything. If it wasn't me under the microscope at a given time, I still felt the same shame and embarrassment by being subjected to listening to her criticism of whoever may be the current offender. In addition to having such a critical spirit, she was also too busy to nurture me and spend quality time with me in an effort to counterbalance all the correcting.

The older I got, the more emotionally distant I became from both her and my family. The distance didn't stop me from trying to win my mother's approval. I was subconsciously protecting myself in this way by working hard around the house. I would deep clean nearly anything in the house. I read more books than you could count in a minute. I accelerated in my schoolwork. That wasn't too difficult, however, because I had been gifted with a natural hunger for education, curiosity, and a knack for understanding new material quickly. My love of learning, coupled with my desire to do well in school to impress my mother, quickly earned me the title of teacher's pet. This peer-given label was deceiving, however, because I often found myself under the disapproving glare of one teacher, or punished with the detention sentence of another or the exasperated sigh of yet another.

This intensified the whole "being an outsider" stigma and very much damaged my prospects of finding a welcoming group. As a preteen girl, coming into the most emotionally and mentally volatile period of a girl's life, I was left with no emotional support or nurturance at home and no worthwhile companions at school.

Sometimes I would make a friend here or there, but none of those relationships ever formed into lasting bonds. Even the friends I did manage to make took great pleasure in teasing me and playing mean tricks on me, devising plans to get me in trouble or hurt.

One such friendship introduced my naive mind to the world of boys, kissing, and sex. I remember the embarrassment I felt at not knowing the answer to the question: "Do you have to take all your clothes off to have sex?" I felt shame and loss of innocence at the ugly remark: "You baby! Of course you don't. I know because I had sex last night and I kept my clothes on." I was only twelve years old when this whispered conversation took place over a computer modem. I hadn't even kissed a boy yet. I hadn't had my first period yet. Imagine my shock when that same girl told me, "You'd better have all the sex you can before you start your period because once you have it, that's when you can get pregnant." These were the kinds of conversations that introduced me to sex and relationships. None of the conversations were kind; they were more like ridicule and peer pressure.

We had stopped going to church with any regularity when my brothers and I grew old enough to be so obnoxious about not wanting to go to church that my mother just gave up trying to make us. By this point we were nearly completely "Christmas-Easter Christians."

One season, during middle school, I attended a church down the road with a neighbor. During that summer, I came home one evening proclaiming that I had been saved! I have no recollection of what prompted my profession of faith that night, but I remember kneeling at the altar as clearly as I remember my mother scoffing at my declaration. She said, "You can't be saved! You don't even know what that means!" Conversely, my dad, in his backslidden state, smiled pitifully and said, "I'm so happy for you!" Sadly, I don't recall going to that church for much longer after that.

In high school, I met my very first boyfriend. He was a dream to me because he looked at me as if he saw me. Adopting my mother's high expectations of me, I became my own worst critic, begging for attention and appreciation in different yet equally obnoxious ways. This immaturity put much strain on my budding relationship with this boy. He, copying the toxic examples of his own parents, was very demeaning to me. He was harsh and negative, causing me to cry quite often. This was my first love, and I was not willing to walk away from this harmful relationship.

I got my first job at sixteen and was a model employee. My managers commended my work and paid me more for doing a good job. This was something I had never experienced before. The more approval I got, the harder I worked to get it. Because I had gotten a job, I was given my grandmother's car. When I got off work, I would go hang out at the local bookstore and interact with some older teenagers and young adults I had known from school. Before I knew it, I was a part of a group that didn't mind me being with them. I started visiting them at their homes, where they would be drinking or using pot. I didn't participate, afraid that my mother would find out I had done some forbidden thing, but I would sit there, not saying a word, thankful no one had asked me to leave.

I developed, partially from my newfound friends and partially from my home life, a cynical attitude, which my boyfriend of two years couldn't accept. After several weeks of vicious arguments, we broke up. Ten nights later, I consoled myself by having sex in the back seat of a car with a boy I hardly knew. I had willingly thrown my virginity out the window. As a matter of fact, that boy, whom I had sought out particularly for his experienced reputation, even asked me if I was sure I knew what I was doing and really wanted to do it. It seemed he cared more about what I was giving away than I did. Everything I had learned about sex completely undermined the value of the gift I so casually threw in the garbage. The fact that this young man slept with another girl two days later drastically and permanently altered my perception of how sex and love should be approached.

From that time on, I lived a double life: perfect little angel when at home or work, and curious, seductive girl on weekends, finding some new boy to razzle-dazzle with my pretty face and slick moves. I began reading *Cosmo* magazine and watching pornography on the sly in an effort to become better at this thrilling new life. Before long, I had gained enough working knowledge that any man would accept my proposition. At first, I dated young men my age. Then I moved on to older men who had more experience and finesse. I always received the very high praise that my broken, hurting little heart needed. During this teenage period of my life, my fights with my mother only escalated. We exchanged nasty, cutting words followed by days of icy silence. My dad gave his best efforts to keep me around the house, either by playing card games, working on projects together, or doing other innocent shenanigans, but the tension between my mother and me was so thick, I would take every opportunity available to leave. Throughout the rest of high school, I spent as little time at home as possible. I worked hard at my job, made spectacular grades at school, and earned the favor of every boy I had a fancy to entertain.

After the heartbreak of my first boyfriend and the other boy who betrayed me, I put up even more walls around my heart. I soon fell into a pattern of finding a boyfriend and having sex with him. The minute the praise for my talents slackened or I became bored or he became clingy, I would dump him and move on to the next challenge. Sometimes I would keep a boyfriend for weeks; sometimes the turnaround was hours. Either way, I got what I needed. I never let myself get into a position to be vulnerable or hurt. I do vividly remember one particularly formative night. I met an older boy who was very aggressive, and although I was scared to have sex with him, I was even more afraid of the anger and rage he would express if I didn't. So for the first time ever, I participated fearfully and reluctantly. Regardless, that experience did not slow me down a bit, and not only did I continue this trend, but also it escalated into my college days.

I had received a full, four-year academic scholarship to a University in Alabama. By this point, I had learned never to ask my parents for money for anything. If I couldn't pay for it myself, I did without. I had no money for field trips, sporting events, clothes or shoes, or any other expense that I didn't earn myself. So when I received this scholarship, I was elated, to put it mildly. The only thing the scholarship didn't cover was my dorm room and my textbooks, which were expenses an aunt and uncle of mine graciously covered as a graduation gift. I set out on my college experience, determined to graduate in four years because I couldn't afford anything else.

My problem was the fact I couldn't decide on an academic major. I had considered elementary education, but I wasn't certain of that, so I changed to business at the last minute because it seemed safer. My course load required me to take fifteen credit hours my first semester and sixteen credit hours the second. The first semester began smoothly. I was attending all my classes, loving learning, and enjoying the freedom that came with being three long hours away from home.

I found a job at a sweet little bookstore and was leading a very happy life. Soon, however, I met a boy at work, and it was not long before I found myself falling into the same patterns as back at home. I started experimenting with alcohol at parties and eventually started smoking pot recreationally. I had tried it once or twice while in high school but was too paranoid and fearful to ever really indulge other than that. A group of friends and I attended football games and partied afterward. I still managed to keep up with my studies, but admittedly, I felt pressure to maintain the grades that were expected of me. I'm not sure who set those unreasonably high expectations: me, my mother, or the university's financial department. I suspect it was mostly me.

The first semester came and went, and I started noticing that I felt unrest. Between working part time, going to school full time, and now living a decent social life, I was stretched very thin. During the spring semester, I started feeling the pressure. I became heavily burdened by the weight of the workload and the knowledge that I could never drop a class because of my four-year deadline. I continued to spend time with friends, sleep around, drink occasionally, and smoke pot. It was a surprise when I realized that smoking pot seemed to help me think more clearly. It almost seemed to help me focus my thoughts and encourage productivity. I managed to work my way through the second semester in this manner, but a few weeks before finals, I cracked.

I suppose I had some form of mental breakdown; I got out of the shower one day, flipped my head over, and, without thinking, cut all my hair off. That same week, I got engaged to a boy whom I had only known for two months. I agreed to this because he was planning to join the Air Force and promised to sign his GI Bill over to me so I could travel with him and finish college at any school I wanted. It didn't even bother me that I thought this boy was incredibly self-centered and immature. He had plans and he was good in bed. In my mentally and emotionally compromised state, that was enough for me.

I was determined to leave college for this boy, but I ended up breaking off the engagement with him before finals were even over. I had missed my registration dates for the next year, so I assumed all the classes I would need to take would already be filled, and my four-year plan was shot. I honestly didn't even check or consult my advisor. I had given up. I somehow managed to pass that semester with flying colors, although I can't understand how I earned myself a spot on the dean's list for the second time.

When I returned home from college, I found myself living much the same life as I lived before, except now, I smoked pot pretty much nonstop. My escapades started dipping into more forbidden territories: having affairs with friends' ex-boyfriends, fiancés, and separated husbands. I found several jobs over the year, here and there, but never pursued anything that might require me to take a drug test. I knew that smoking pot did something to my brain that helped me to navigate life differently, but I never had a desire to try harder drugs.

I don't know if it was because of the raw situations I put myself in at such a pivotal time in life, or the emotional neglect I struggled with as a child, but during my early teenage years, I started to notice that the way I felt emotions was different somehow. At certain times the emotions I experienced would become more pronounced and harder to handle. When I was sixteen, my gynecologist wrote me a prescription for Prozac. I refused to take it because I had heard terrible things about this drug, and I didn't want to be a vegetable for the rest of my life. Therefore, I continued to struggle with my emotions, depression, and anxiety for years, until I started smoking pot. Marijuana became my miracle drug. My new home life included working odd jobs as well as continuing to be sexually active. I desperately needed someone to accept me, but no matter how hard I tried, those needs weren't fulfilled.

Though I continued to smoke more pot, I eventually got a job at Books-A-Million and loved working there. For some reason, I decided to shoplift a few doors down in the strip mall. I had done this before, usually with friends in high school, but I had never gotten caught. I got caught this time and ended up going to jail for the first time ever. Though I only stayed in the police station for about three hours while I waited for my dad to bail me out, the situation scared me half to death, humiliated me, and broke my heart. On top of that, I lost a job I loved so incredibly much.

Because of my choices, I was forced to find yet another job. I accepted a position as a telemarketer at a fundraising office for different charities. The majority of employees were women from all walks of life, and the only men who worked there were the two bosses. I was successful at my job and earned high praise for it too. I joined a group of girls at work who used drugs as well. As we became close, we smoked pot before work and on lunch breaks and came back to continue with our calls. It seemed like the perfect setup, even though some of the girls were super sketchy. It was obvious they did more than smoke pot. One day at lunch, a girl brought out a container of pills. She and another girl in the car crushed the pills and snorted them. I had never seen anyone do that. One of the girls offered me a try, but I had no desire to sniff anything up my nose. As time passed, it was almost like show-and-tell at lunch: the girls brought their drugs of choice to the car, divvied them up, and consumed them. I accepted different pain and nerve pills to try out. Afterward, we would all go back to the phones and bring in sales to a campaign manager.

Our office was an open space, and the main boss sat at a desk near mine. We would chat in between calls, and at first our relationship stayed professional. Though we had each other's phone numbers, we only texted one another over work-related issues. Things changed, and we began talking about things beyond work. I was developing an intellectual attraction to him, but he seemed to want something more intimate. I knew he was married at the time and had four children, but I asked him to meet me outside of work to talk. Within a week, we were sleeping together, initiating an affair that lasted several months. During this time, I moved out of my parents' house and into an apartment with one of the girls I worked with. I was living my best life, or so I thought, doing drugs with my roommate and sleeping with my boss. As a sideline to pay for what we wanted to smoke, we started selling weed. My roommate often invited old friends to buy weed and visit with us. When one of the guys, Toby, expressed an interest in me, I told him that I was in a very dark place mentally and had nothing to offer him at present.

Notwithstanding, Toby became my party buddy. We would drink and smoke and take pills. I did it all to try to escape my emotional torment. One night, in a drugged stupor, I had sex with him. Though I continued to hang out and party with him, I didn't have sex with him again until several weeks later on my twenty-first birthday. Ten days after that, I discovered I was seven weeks pregnant, and I had no idea which of these horrible men had gotten me pregnant. I was so incredibly devastated and scared and mad. I was even more upset when shortly after finding out I was pregnant, I learned that both my boss and party buddy were meth addicts. My emotional turmoil continued for several months while I tried to find a way out of my situation. I ended my affair with my boss and quit talking to my party buddy. Unfortunately, I couldn't quit my job and search for another because I was four months pregnant at this point. The unprofessional atmosphere at work was the perfect environment for all sorts of rumors and derision to grow, and I spent a large portion of my workday hiding in the bathroom crying and fighting back nausea.

Days before I found out I was pregnant, I had moved into my own apartment. So after work, I would come home, alone and brokenhearted. I finally quit that job when I was about six months pregnant. I was able to pressure my boss into firing me, which enabled me to draw unemployment. I didn't know it at the time, but God was blessing my decision to quit my job. While visiting a friend the weekend after I quit, my car was hit in a parking lot. There wasn't much damage, but the insurance company decided

I was due a check for $837. I was so relieved; God was taking care of me financially. I was incredibly happy to be out of the toxic wasteland that was my life.

Surprisingly, God continued to bless me. A few weeks later, while taking a walk with my mother in her neighborhood, we discovered a little house down the street was being renovated. We walked up and spoke to the owner, who, after giving us further details of the house, agreed to let me rent it for only a few dollars more a month than my current apartment rent payment. To make matters even more humbling, a few weeks after that, an aunt threw me a baby shower. As I was leaving, she handed me an envelope containing a check for three months of my rent. I could not believe all these good things that were happening to me. I got moved into the peaceful little house one month before my son was born.

Two weeks before his birth, I was sitting on my parents' porch, telling my dad I had not spoken to the baby's father almost my entire pregnancy. Furthermore, I told my dad that I had no intention of including the baby's father in our lives. Earlier I had confided to my mother that I didn't know who the baby's dad actually was, but I hadn't shared that with my father. What he told me on the porch, however, completely changed my mind. My dad told me that no matter how terrible the baby's father actually was, my son deserved to know his dad. It took me a while to decide to call Toby, but after a week I called him and invited him to lunch. We discussed the fact that he might indeed be the baby's father, and we talked about the necessity of a DNA test. I told Toby that if he would pay for the DNA test and it revealed that he was in fact the baby's father, I would let him be part of the baby's life, but only on my terms. He agreed to all those conditions, and I agreed to call him when I went into labor.

The next week, my doctor determined I was in labor and sent me to the hospital. I called Toby, who came up to the hospital as soon as he could. It was a little awkward, but the birth of that precious baby blessed all of us. After the baby and I got home and settled in, Toby came over, and we did a DNA test on him and my son. Finally, after what felt like an eternity, the results were in: Toby was in fact the father of this precious baby child! Once we knew the results, I allowed him to come visit the baby a few times a week. Anytime I called, he would come, freshly showered and clothed, bringing money or diapers—every single time. I didn't make it easy on him: I would randomly call him and tell him he could see the baby for one hour if he came to my house immediately. Every time, he would drop whatever he was doing and spend every minute I would let him with his son. He would also leave as soon as I asked him to and never complained. It was during these visits that I really had an opportunity to get to know my son's father.

When the baby was about five weeks old, during one of our visits, Toby told me he had been attending church nearby, where he told his friends that he had a son. It was his biggest wish to take his son to church to meet these people. He assured me, however, that I did not have to go. No mother is going to let a five-week-old baby out of her sight, so the following Sunday I attended a new church for the very first time. I had been raised to believe that the Baptist church was nothing but hypocrites and heathens. The contemporary-music-playing, hand-clapping, and hand-raising church was so different than the holy, reverent, ritualistic church I had grown up in, and it made me extremely uncomfortable.

The biweekly baby visits continued, enabling Toby and me to become good friends. When I decided to go back to school in January, I felt comfortable enough to ask Toby to move in with me and be my roommate. I was hoping we could coparent together. There was no more work available at his job, so between his unemployment checks and my student loans, we made enough money to pay our bills for several months. Because of this, I went back to school full time and he kept the baby. We were strictly roommates: we had separate bedrooms, separate shelves in the pantry, everything.

During all this time I never stopped smoking pot. I had cut back significantly when I was pregnant, but I never fully quit; as soon as the baby was born, I started smoking regularly again. I would never smoke to the point of being stoned or unable to function, but I stayed high enough all day long. Marijuana enabled me to perform my school duties and keep my thoughts focused when I started back to school. During one of my school research projects on different illnesses, I began to suspect I have ADHD. After researching further for the project, I sought medical help. My doctor told me there was no need to run tests because he could clearly see I did in fact have ADHD. He wrote me a prescription for Adderall and required me to come see him a month later. Additionally, he told me I had to quit smoking pot, or it could cost him his license. I agreed to his conditions. The medication helped me focus my thoughts, but it also made me angry, and I hated the way the medicine made me feel. Among other side effects, I was unable to carry on conversations with Toby that didn't end in nasty fights, so I made the decision to stop taking Adderall and to continue smoking pot.

A few months into the semester, my relationship with Toby turned romantic, and a few months later we started going to church together. Soon, I began feeling convicted that Toby and I were living in sin. I just didn't feel right about something, and I decided the solution was that we either needed to stop living together or we needed to get married. One evening as we were sitting in a bar, I proposed to him, and he said yes. A few months later, we got married, and the very next week I was calling divorce lawyers, trying to find a way out of the marriage; the strong something-is-wrong feeling had not gone away when we said, "I do."

We continued to live together and attend church faithfully, hardly missing a Sunday or Wednesday service. A few months later at a Wednesday-night Bible study, the pastor asked, "If you were to die right now, do you know for sure that you would go to heaven?" My chest grew tight because I didn't know. Sure, I was doing better than what I had been doing. I was keeping a lot of the rules in the Bible, but I didn't know for sure that I would go to heaven. I realized that though I had plenty of knowledge of Jesus by this point, I didn't actually have a personal relationship with Him. I went to the altar, and a sweet little lady noticed my shaking hands. She opened her Bible and showed me several verses that I had heard many times before. She asked me, "Now do you know?" I said, "Uh, yeah!" She said, "Great! You're saved. Let's pray!" So I said a prayer that night with that lady at the altar.

It wasn't until several weeks later that the meat of the Gospel message settled down in my heart and I accepted the free gift of salvation. I realized and trusted that Christ had died for *me* on that cross, not just for all humanity, and that no amount of work on my part could get me into heaven. The work Christ had already done on the cross, and my acceptance of that gift and submission to His authority, was the only thing that could get me to heaven.

At that moment, I surrendered my life in the best way that I could, to Him. The conviction that worried me so much completely went away. My life started changing in very subtle but noticeable ways after that. Over time I started noticing more joy in myself. Peace. Patience with Toby and others around me. Other promised fruits of the spirit that only come from living in relationship with Jesus, fruits that I had tried so desperately to obtain myself before I gave my heart to God. I started to see that even though I wasn't perfect, God wasn't giving up on me. Jesus was continuing to grow me and mold me and slowly change me from the inside out. I started noticing over time that it was becoming easier to live out His biblical commands and I didn't have to try so hard. Even when I made mistakes, God was still in the middle of the mess with me, showing me how to make it right. Over time, God was helping me understand that He wouldn't leave me and that He delights in me. No matter how many wrong turns I take or how many times I pout in stubborn, immature defiance, He is steadfastly and sweetly still pushing me on toward the mark He has set for me.

God has forgiven me for all the terrible things I have done in my past. He has forgiven me for all the hateful words I have spoken or even just thought. He has given me an eternal residence in heaven and a Holy Spirit promise of eternal fellowship with my heavenly Father. He also has many amazing blessings that He wants me to enjoy here on earth. God began a purifying work in me that is still ongoing today, eight and a half years later. He is working to heal me from deep-seated emotional wounds and rewiring my brain from all the terrible things I have seen and done. God is reminding me of my worth in Him. He is tempering my spirit to treat others with the same love and kindness Jesus does. God is not only trying to rewrite how I view myself, but also how I view what others think about me. He doesn't want me to work to earn His delight in me. His love is not something I have to earn. His love is not conditional.

He has also brought restoration in the relationships in my earthly family. He has allowed for great healing to happen and Holy Spirit forgiveness to extend into situations that could not be touched otherwise. I can be free to accept whatever amount of love, with whatever conditions, my earthly family has to offer, because of the security I have in the love God has displayed toward me through Christ. The sweetest part to consider is He has grown my family. Toby and I now have four of our own precious children, whom I can nurture and pour love upon. God has given me a husband who loves me, but who loves God more and continually seeks to follow His lead the best he can.

Christ saved me so I can experience an awesome intimate fellowship with Him in my life. I experience His tender forgiveness when I mess up. I enjoy all the blessings He pours down on my life. I depend upon Him to navigate through life's difficulties and uncertainties, because even when the storms rage around me and the seasons change, He is steadfast.

SAFETY

Safety

He leaves one way and comes home changed. As he works to feed his habits, drugs and alcohol consume his life. Through his time in the military, divorces, and homelessness, he is looking for an answer. One man is looking for his identity only to find that his identity is in the safety of his heavenly Father.

When I was four, my life was turned upside down, though I didn't understand what was happening and just thought it was normal. My sister and her new husband, who had moved to Texas from Alabama, had come back home for a visit. They invited me to return with them for a visit and convinced my mother they would take care of me. Mom agreed, and I went home with them to Texas. While I was there things happened that would forever change my life. I was left at home alone while my sister and her husband went to work during the day, making me feel all alone in the world. But the worst was the fact I was molested by my brother-in-law. Yet I told no one. I was not the same little boy when I returned home.

I never said anything to anyone, and no one ever asked if anything happened. As I grew older, my father was always angry and abusive—verbally and physically. This continued until my father passed away when I was ten years old. After my dad passed away, my sister gave me my first beer, which caused my later addiction. I never mentioned the sexual abuse because I thought that was the way things were, and people didn't talk about that. My brother had married a woman whose son was just a little older than I. We had the same early life, with adults taking advantage of him as they had me. These shared experiences made it easy for us to have sexual relations. We were seeking comfort and acceptance, but eventually we grew apart in our teenage years.

I started working at the age of fourteen, and by sixteen, I had a steady job at McDonald's. That helped me afford my addiction, as well as clothes and my own car. On weekends when I closed the restaurant, I would join my coworkers at someone's house to party until morning. This happened almost every weekend. My parents were negligent and never questioned the things I did. It was obvious no one cared about me. I was able to do whatever I wanted without any consequences. I was raising myself.

At the age of eighteen, looking for someone to love me for me, I decided to marry my high school sweetheart the day after graduation. It was a disaster because neither of us understood the difference between lust and love. Earlier I had joined the National Guard, and following graduation, I was sent to basic training for the army. I had hoped this would turn my life around, but I was sadly mistaken. While I was in advanced individual training, which provides training for specific jobs in the army, I was drinking more than ever and even passed out in the enlisted club on post. Again, I remember drinking so much that I passed out while I was dancing. A couple of friends helped me out of the building to get some air and to sober up enough to walk back to the barracks. A kind military police officer came by and gave me a ride back to my barracks. Fortunately, I was able to avoid any problem before I graduated from the program.

Following my graduation, I returned home and tried to straighten out my life. My wife and I attended church, where I got saved and baptized. I was even able to get a job working in a fast-food restaurant. Unfortunately, this boring lifestyle wasn't enough for me. To take part in something more challenging, I signed up for active duty in the army and was stationed in Germany. Germany is well known for its beer, and life in the military lends itself to drinking. My wife had accompanied me to Germany, but because she was pregnant, she stayed six months before going back to the States. When our daughter was born, I was able to get leave and visit my family for a short time. I returned to Germany and experienced my first high with LSD. The army has a strict drug test protocol, but I never took one test. One of my friends was in charge of the testing and helped me avoid getting caught.

I fulfilled my obligation in Germany and was sent to Texas. While I was in Texas, I got a divorce from my wife. In Texas, the army base was located near the Mexico border, providing easy access to inexpensive drugs. Friends and I would cross the border and spend weekends in Mexico. My drug usage helped me to escape reality as well as other problems I was facing. One night, in a drunken stupor, I crashed my car into a light pole. The consequence of this accident was that the east side of town was darkened for hours. The army, being what it is, took jurisdiction of the DUI from the local police department and kept it in-house. After this, I did not have a civilian record of a DUI, but the army placed all this information in my file.

Shortly after this incident, the army discharged me, and I decided to move to follow my friend to Maine. There I hit the party scene and married a party friend of mine who was currently pregnant with another man's child. I adopted that young girl in 1998. Unfortunately, our marriage went downhill. The verbal abuse from our fighting drove me into a deep depression.

In 1999, my wife became pregnant and gave birth to our son. I hoped that this would be a way to possibly save our marriage because I would have done anything at that time to make it work.

However, we were having trouble paying bills, and there was an additional mouth to feed, which didn't help the situation. We had moved to New Hampshire just before our son was born. Though my wife had been dealing with alcohol issues before the move, she now used alcohol to a greater extent. She couldn't even take good care of the children, and I had to quit working to take care of all of them. My wife's brother offered us a place to live if we agreed to move back to Maine. We tried to make things work, but soon we were separated.

I had to leave home, so my wife drove me to Portland, where I slept behind a dumpster for a couple of days and finally found a homeless shelter. I had to start over, and with the help of HUD housing, I found a place to rent. I was able to find a job, but I had to walk nine miles one way to do overnight stocking at a grocery store. With the money left over after I paid for rent and food as well as child support, I eased my mental pain with alcohol.

My wife and I tried to get back together several times, but our efforts failed because we were both drinking heavily. We argued, and my wife revealed shocking truths. She bragged about the fact she had extramarital affairs, which caused a full-blown screaming match. She picked up a plate and threw it at me. Dodging the plate, I grabbed her and put her in a headlock that almost put her to sleep. Stunned, I let her go. She called the police, who took me to jail for assault. I was separated from the children for four months until my wife brought the little ones around so I could see them.

In 2001 we settled our differences and became a family again. During this time my wife's oldest brother moved to Florida and invited me to help him move for some extra money. I really liked this small city in northern Florida, and felt this new location would help restore our relationship. Fortunately, I happened to find a job and felt a move here would help us get away from the North and leave all our problems.

The move didn't meet my expectations. Because of my wife's continual drinking, she was placed in rehab. During the time leading up to my wife's rehab, I lost my job because I had to care for the children. The children and I spent a lot of time together. We took the bus into downtown, where we got on a train that took us all over town. The children loved this, and the tram itself was air-conditioned, giving us a chance to be cool.

Soon, my second wife and I divorced.

The ensuing years almost followed a pattern. I found a well-paid job with a pest-control company. One of the workers offered me a room to rent and allowed my children to visit. Unfortunately, he also became my drug supplier. I would pick up kilos of cocaine to break down and help distribute. I had to find a new place to rent after I was harassed by buyers with guns. Due to the rental prices and my lack of money, I was forced to buy a tent to live in. Every two weeks I had to move my tent to a different park because of the parks' rules.

During this time, my kids visited me. Although they thought sleeping in a tent was fun, I wanted to find a real place for us to stay while they visited. However, tent living did save me a lot of money, and I was then able to rent a room for a few months. That was better than the tent when my kids visited me. Soon, though, my drug-buying habit left me with no money, which led me to leave the rental and move into my tent again. This was becoming a vicious cycle, and much to my embarrassment, it became a running joke among my coworkers.

Seeking fulfillment and answers to questions, I turned to witchcraft. I read books about spells and charms, hoping to ease my pain, embarrassment, and shame. I was sure I could find answers to life questions in these pages, but I failed to find any satisfactory answers. During this time, I bought a car for $500, and I used it to pick up drugs from my dealer's house. To keep from paying the car's registration, I switched my car tag with the tag off my work truck. One night, however, I ran a red light. A policeman pulled me over and wrote a ticket, and I spent an entire week in jail. Because of this, I missed my son's eighth birthday party, which broke my heart. I knew I was at a turning point. I finally had to make a decision to do something with my life. I was either going to die or go to jail for a very long time if I continued living this way, and I couldn't face prison or death. After I begged and pleaded with my parents, they finally came down to Florida and took me home to Alabama. I was able to connect with my daughter whom I hadn't seen in a long time, but I was leaving my other two children behind in Florida.

I chose to start a new life in Alabama, hoping to see my other children again in the future. I chose to try to detox at my parents' home because I didn't have money for a rehabilitation center. My parents asked me to chop up a large tree that had fallen in their yard. I used the exercise of chopping the tree and cutting it up for firewood to sell to aid my detox. The two weeks it took me to accomplish this task enabled me to deal with the loss of my children and the destructive life I had chosen for myself. I found that I was able to stop using drugs.

Shortly after, I began attending church with my daughter. There I found quiet strength and hope. Soon I surrendered my life to Christ, in January 2008. After this, my life started to improve. My church family supported me in my faith, and I became close to a special family. These people took me under their wings, asked how I was doing, and cared about my life. I had never experienced such unconditional love. Because of my former life, it was awkward to accept their generosity and love at first; then I realized this is the relationship I always had longed for. I was accepted for who I am, and I will never forget that feeling.

Later, I married a strong woman who was also a recovering

drug addict and alcoholic. Because I had found an excellent job, we were able to buy a home in 2008, but higher child support payments forced us to move into a house on my parents' property. This house was a gift from God. We didn't have house payments and were able to remodel the house, where we lived for many years.

My wife, now a dedicated Christian, and I were very involved in ministries at church. It was a joy for me. Looking back, I was proud of what I had accomplished and forgot God was the instrument of my change. My great pride cost me my fellowship with God; I had lost that vital connection with Him.

Continuing to be a super Christian on the outside, I was going through rapid change on the inside. My feelings of depression became anger because God was convicting me to change, but I was looking for strength in all the wrong places. I was primed for a relapse, and my craving for cocaine resurfaced. My wife's son had a medical condition requiring him to take medicine for attention-deficit/hyperactivity disorder, or ADHD. I was aware that the medication produced a high similar to cocaine, and I started taking it and replacing the capsules with aspirin. Because the aspirin did nothing to help her son, my wife was convinced there was a problem with the drug company and pharmacy.

My deepening depression led me to attempt suicide in November 2013. My wife thought my worsening condition was caused by my regular medication and rushed me to the US Department of Veterans Affairs hospital emergency room so I could get my meds adjusted. She was unaware of the fact that I had really swallowed a handful of antidepressant meds. I wished to die in the car or the hospital so my wife wouldn't have memories of my death at home, but my suicide attempt failed. The kind of medication I took would only put me in a coma, not kill me. I couldn't even get *that* right.

My memories of everything in my childhood, the army, and my

past marriages caused my psychotic break. After I woke up, I spent three weeks in a VA psychiatric hospital. After I was able to return home, I continued counseling at the VA. I was miserable because my marriage was in trouble. I had little money for Christmas because I had lost my income during my three-week stay in the hospital. Luckily, though, the owner of the company reinstated me, and I was able to work after I left the hospital. God provided for us through kind people who donated Christmas gifts to our son. We were blessed by God and people with generous hearts.

A couple of weeks after Christmas, I broke down and took more of my wife's son's medication. I finally realized I was going to need further rehabilitation. I had to wait three weeks to enter a Christian-based rehab in South Carolina. A friend of ours had opened a homeless shelter in Georgia, and the person who ran it invited me to come and stay there. Both these programs were free, enabling me to leave Alabama so I could concentrate on my recovery. I knew I was God's missing sheep and was determined to stay there until He healed me. I had a new sense of God in my life and a new understanding of life in general. I returned home a completely new man, dedicated to God and family.

God had restored me. My wife became my best friend again, and we worked at becoming a loving, committed couple. Under God's leadership, I was able to find a rewarding job. God had provided a way not only to take care of my family but also to restore our commitment. I was able to turn my life around as far as drugs and alcohol were concerned. Now, I am totally free of my addictions.

Many individuals believe God would not allow His people to go through depression or suicidal thoughts, because they forget that God gives us free will. God's plan is that all His creation will come to know Him and follow His will; however, many will choose to reject Him and His will in our lives. I thank God for allowing me to go through things that would change my perspective: He enabled me to change my attitude toward serving Him and serving others. He enabled both my wife and me to restore our relationship to a level we never thought possible. Because of this, we are still in ministry and still involved in church. We live a sanctified life now.

My life verse is Isaiah 26:3 (KJV): "Thou will keep him in perfect peace, whose mind is stayed on thee: because he trusteth in thee." I have to keep my focus on God, or I lose focus on everything else. Is every day rosy and great? No! But is every day bearable? Absolutely! I know without a doubt Christ is fighting for me every day. I know there is One who sticks closer to me than a brother. I am reminded Christ is good enough for me. God sent His Son to die on the cross for me and for you! I have safety and comfort knowing that in every situation that I may find myself, Christ is with me. Whenever the devil reminds me of my past to shame me, I know that beyond a shadow of a doubt I'm forgiven. The things in our past should keep us humble, not broken. Our past and forgiveness can serve as an inspiration to others who have lost their way. There is joy in knowing that God will use our past to bless someone in our future. As stated in 1 Corinthians 1:4 (KJV): "Who comforteth us in all our tribulation, that we may be able to comfort them which are in any trouble, by the comfort wherewith we ourselves are comforted of God."

■ ENOUGH

Enough ∎

She thinks it is all her fault and never knows her true identity. She looks to numb all her pain through any escape she can find. Remembering only a glimpse of unconditional love from distant family, she moves to a new place to start over. She finds an altar and prays. As she realizes that God is enough for her and she is not His, she finds that no other last name is needed.

I t's hard to bare your soul to someone new, but I truly believe that the life I have lived was for a purpose far beyond the pain. Maybe you are another me, and this story will tell you about Someone who is far greater than any pain anyone has ever endured.

I grew up in Florida in a family where God didn't exist. My mom and dad split when I was three. She was gone—no cards, letters, calls, or visits. My brother and I were raised by my dad. Dad remarried several times, and with each new stepmother, I experienced a buffet style of abuse that no one, let alone a child, should ever have to experience.

He married stepmother number one when I was four. When I think back, my mind seems to block out a lot, and, other than what I vividly remember, the rest runs together. Being scared to leave my bed and being laughed at while I cried were things I do remember. One day my stepmother held me by my feet, swung me around, and kicked me in the stomach and head. During this episode my father came home, saw what was happening, and quickly came to my rescue. Miraculously, he caught me in midair and took me to my bedroom and placed me on my bed. There was a terrible commotion in the living room, after which my stepmother left and never returned. Sometime later, sitting directly across from my dad, I noticed he was distracted. He seemed angry and began drawing figures of people on a piece of paper. I was amazed at the picture, but it only lasted a quick moment because my dad tore it straight down the middle. He looked directly at me and said, "I hope you are happy." He indicated my stepmom leaving was all my fault. To this day every time I taste blood in my mouth, I am reminded of swinging upside down and thinking it was all my fault.

I was seven when my father married stepmom number two. Unfortunately, she had a serious drug addiction. Neither my brother nor I got to celebrate holidays. There were celebrations, however, when our stepmom decided to give up her drug habit. We all celebrated when she flushed her pills down the toilet as a sign of her serious intention—until Dad found her hidden stash of pills. Then we had to listen to the arguments that ensued. I admit I lay on my floor and recorded their arguments with my tape recorder. When my parents were not at home, I listened to the recordings over and over because they would keep me company since I felt so alone.

Around the age of nine, I remember hearing a loud crash of broken glass in my parents' bedroom. They had been fighting for a while, and I was terrified something terrible had happened. I ran barefoot into their room and stepped on the broken glass that covered their floor. The pain was indescribable. I screamed not only because of the pain, but also because my dad was on top of her on the edge of the bed, holding her down. He had to restrain her because she had been hitting him. Her fists were balled so tight they were bone white. I couldn't believe they were her hands. My stepmom called the cops, accusing my dad of physical abuse, and they came and took my dad away as my brother and I cried to him to come back.

After he left, my brother and I were terribly angry and ached for his return. Our stepmother became angry because we were so upset. She screamed at me to just be quiet, and when my brother tried to protect me and tell her to leave me alone, she quickly backhanded him across the face. His nose was bleeding. Like it was yesterday, I can see him slouched at the foot of his bunk bed with tear-filled eyes. Though the front of his shirt and face were covered in blood, he was so angry that he wouldn't even wipe the blood away.

Four days later, my dad came home. He sat us down and told us he wanted to work on his marriage. To protect us, he asked us how we felt about foster care and living with another family for a while. During this time, he said stepmom number two was having a tough time, and it wasn't fair to just give up on her.

That night I asked if I could find my birth mother and go live with her instead of some stranger. I longed for my mother and the chance for change. I was sure she would take me back. At that point in my life, I would have traded my life for any other. Surprisingly, my father was able to find my biological mother quickly. I hadn't even heard from her for six years. Within one week, I was on a plane headed to Connecticut to live with her and her new family. Little did I know that in exchange for the life I thought was killing me, I traded for a life that was even worse. In addition, my dad found some relatives and friends that would take in my brother.

Strict parenting was not even close to what began happening to me in my mom's home. My stepfather beat my back and legs black and blue because I couldn't read the clocks that weren't digital. Then he beat me because I didn't know which last name to use. Was I Michelle Henry (dad's last name), Sabb (mom number one), Camilla (mom number two), or Breklyn (mom number three)?

There were so many people in and out of my life, I think I simply forgot who I was along the way.

The beatings weren't the biggest problem, because my stepfather started molesting me. I didn't want to wear a skirt, knowing he would just lift it up anyways. He would lick my face and make me do things, so I refused to say goodnight to him. I didn't want to get out of bed in the morning due to the fact he had just left my room an hour before. I was so confused. I knew it was wrong from the very beginning; all of it was so wrong. Day after day, night after night, I would lie in bed with him and play dead while I would silently beg for the breath to leave my body. I just wanted to die right there in front of him. I was already dying a little each day.

My dad eventually called. Though I hadn't talked to him the whole time I was gone, all I could do was sob and beg for him to let me come home. I couldn't bring myself to say why. Why I needed him, why I had to leave, why I was so scared. Unfortunately, he told me he was still busy working on his marriage and offered to send me to my grandmother's home in Maine.

My Mimi and Aunt Olivia were the source of the only relief I had in my ten years. With them I experienced two years of the warmest love and best French toast this world could offer. I know they saved my life. They showed me that not everything in the world was as ugly as it had been. Even if they never learned the truth, they loved me with a quiet, still, unconditional, painless love I had never known before.

When my grandmother's and aunt's health started to fail when I was twelve, Dad brought me back home, and my brother returned home too. Dad was still working on mending the last marriage. Nothing had changed except we were older. That meant the fights were louder because we yelled back and began to fight back. There were more bloody noses and black eyes as well as threats of broken bones. We often ran away or were forced out of the house weekly. We always returned.

At the age of thirteen, I found my first escape through drugs. For the first time ever, I was numb; nothing mattered. I began smoking pot, then moved to acid and ecstasy. Before I knew it, nine years had passed, and I had indulged in everything that had been offered me, just trying to fade away. Those nine years were a blur. During this time, I was raped. During this terrible event I had a flashback: it was as if I were nine years old again being attacked by my stepfather. So I lay lifeless, begging for the breath to leave my body. After I tried to overdose on a bottle of pills, I was dozing in and out of consciousness, and I remember seagulls flying outside the window. I begged for my breath to fly away like the seagulls. Why couldn't I just fade away, cease to exist? Why couldn't I just die? I spent years numb, attempting to fill a void and feed a hunger that seemed endless. The feeling of emptiness was louder than any other voice I had ever heard. But it was with me daily.

I was in a relationship when I became pregnant at age twenty-two. Throughout the pregnancy, I continued to use drugs. But, keep in mind, to me, to the world, I was nothing, just a strung-out druggy. With the pregnancy, I was expected to be something to this tiny baby. All I could think of was how much better he would be without me. In the early months of my son's life, drug use and depression brought me to the brink of suicide. I went into the bathroom, clutching a razor blade, staring at myself in the mirror: I had a decision to make because my baby was still young enough that it wouldn't matter if I lived or died. My decision, however, changed when I heard him stirring in his bed. I set the blade down and walked away. However, I would come back to the blade when my rent money came up missing; after arguments and fighting; after being told I was replaceable, ugly, and worthless; and when my stash ran dry and I had to feel. I would go back to the blade, the blade that never left the sink.

When my son celebrated his first birthday, I knew he could not live without me and I could not live without him. Finally, I stopped going back to the blade. Moreover, I wanted to stop having a reason to go back. I wanted to stop being me. I wanted to be someone different. I wanted to leave and never return. I decided to create a new life for my son and me. I chose a place I had never been, a place where no one would know me. I chose Alabama. I had an opportunity for people to expect good of me instead of worthlessness. It was not even for me at this point. I needed to give my son a chance to grow up with a kind of love I only had glimpsed. The quiet, still, unconditional, painless love I had glimpsed in Maine.

This was a time of change for my dad as well. Dad had met someone new, someone who was good for him. She was a woman who radiated selfless love and caring. She loved me as a mother should. Here was the person I wanted to be for my child. My bad habits didn't change overnight; I was still a drug addict. Unfortunately, it was the only life I knew. It was easy for me to find drugs. I even started to get high again. I was numb, not angry. I was lost. I was in a place, despite the nearness of my father and his wife, where no one knew me and the struggles I was trying to overcome.

A year later, a man walked into my life. He was kind and told me he was a recovering addict. He had moved to this town to start over. His goal, he told me, was to become a better person than he had been for so long. Looking at him and listening to his confident plans, I began to see the person that I, too, could become. Here was proof that I could change and start over. I knew it could work. By the way, God did change him, and one day he would become my husband. Within weeks, I stopped drinking, smoking, and doing drugs. I was on my way to a better life. I knew it would be difficult and it required hard work, but I was ready. I accepted an invitation to church, and this is where I found answers to my questions. I had often wondered, "Who is this God that is so great? How can He forgive me for all I've done? If He exists, why has no one told me about Him?"

In December 2008, God changed my life. During church that morning, the preacher gave an invitation to come to the altar. When I knelt at the altar, an altar worker asked what I needed God to do in my life. I whispered the only word I could manage—*everything*. There was no other word more fitting. At that moment God took me—broken, torn, bruised, scarred—and made me brand new. He filled me with so much love and joy in a single moment that I couldn't even speak. All I could do was sob. He also surrounded me with a church family who immediately loved me unconditionally. Before they asked who I was or where I had come from, they said they loved me. I felt their love, and it was good.

Over the last few years, God has given me a love that is more powerful than my memories, though I still remember them. Now, I am stronger because of Him. I have learned that God doesn't make bad things happen. We were just born into a sin-cursed world. I knew that God, my heavenly Father, had intentions for my life: He intended for my story to be used. He intended for the breath to never leave my body, He intended for me to cherish what it felt like to be loved, and He also intended for me to go back into the world that was so cruel to me to tell everyone about Him. He did this so that one day, when I meet another me, I can tell that person of a Father's love so great and powerful that it won't matter who they are. That if they accept Jesus and all He has to offer, He will meet them where they are. I can tell them that my God can turn all the ugly in life to beauty. No matter how broken we come to Him, we can be made brand new.

Although, no matter how changed I am, times can still get hard. The difference now is that God has kept me by His side, sometimes even carrying me when I had nothing left to give. Today, it feels good to say I am someone new. My dad and I are mending our relationship, and I know that he is sorry for my childhood. I have learned to forgive him, my birth mother, and a few others along the way. Most importantly, I have learned to forgive myself. That was probably the hardest of all to do.

I have done my share of asking for forgiveness in return and working hard daily to be the mom my growing boy deserves. My husband and I are raising him in a home filled with purpose, forgiveness, and Godly love. I have found a desire inside me that I had always been too numb to feel and a purpose that is so fulfilling. It makes the story itself worth all the heartache in my life, and I am thankful that my breath never left my body.

Because as hard, sad, and scary as the past was, I *lived* my life. I'm responsible for everything I did and survived everything that was done to me. I am proud to say that a part of me finally died, and I was born into a new life. John 11:25 (KJV) states: "Jesus said unto her, I am the resurrection, and the life: he that believeth in me, though he were dead, yet shall he live." I look back through the years, and I can see now where God was waiting for me to discover Him in that chaos. Through it all, He never gave up on me. I understand that life may not always seem fair or easy, yet my story isn't over. I know life will never be what it used to be because now I have a guide, Someone who sacrificed everything so that I can be His. Because now, the Holy Spirit lives in me. I have hope, I am loved, I am His.

GRACE

Grace ▪

His life revolves around alcohol and empty promises. He goes
to rehab and soon finds himself divorced. He is a man lost
in alcohol who discovers the grace of Jesus Christ.

I'm a southern boy who grew up in Alabama in a Christian
home. Church was the focus of our lives, except for my dad,
who was an alcoholic. Mom was the strong influence in our
lives and saw to it that we faithfully attended church. Because
alcohol was readily available in our home, I had my first drink
when I was eight years old. Though I didn't like the taste, I would
sneak a drink every now and then. When I was twelve, my parents
got a divorce, and I was devastated. Like many children, I thought
the divorce was my fault. Because my parents had joint custody of
me, I spent alternate weekends with my dad and was able to sneak
more drinks.

When I was thirteen, sitting with my friends in church, I
realized I was the only one who was not saved. When the altar
call was announced, I went to the altar to pray, but my heart
didn't change. Though I was always involved in church, the
older I got, the more I failed to go. By the time I was sixteen,
my family and I stopped attending church altogether. In high
school, I started hanging out with older friends, partying on the
weekends, and running around with girls. As a senior in high

93

school, I got a job and had more money, enabling me to party and drink more often.

I never caused trouble. Although I was a fun drunk, I was always responsible. Even when I attended all-night parties, I never used the drugs that were available. Because college was an all-the-time party, my grades were failing. Following that, a group of older men invited me to join their softball team. Playing softball was fun, and after our games, we would sit around and drink.

I didn't quit drinking after the season. In fact, by then, I was drinking even more. By the time I was twenty-one, I was an alcoholic but not drinking every day. New bars and clubs opened up, so I could go anywhere I wanted and buy my own beer. The next year, I moved in with a friend. Because I didn't have to answer to anyone, we held our own parties. The parties attracted not only guys but also women. Everything was going great until the police broke up a party and I was taken to jail. Partying was over at our house. After some time passed, I got a job where all my friends worked. It was a perfect setup. On the way to the job site, we would pick up beer, and coming back to clock out, we would pick up more beer. Another opportunity to make money came when my boss offered to pay me to drive us back and forth for beer runs. I also played in another softball league. My addiction escalated.

When I was thirty, I met a lady at our league game. We dated for six months and decided to live together. She had a three-year-old son who wanted to go everywhere with me. Though I was still drinking, I promised my girlfriend I would stop drinking when we got married. My mom and my friends warned my girlfriend that I couldn't stop my addiction and not to expect my compliance. The next summer, however, she wanted to get married. So I met her at the courthouse, and we were married at a civil ceremony. That night, I played softball, and she came to watch. Despite my promise, I did not stop drinking.

I told my wife I had another plan: I would stop drinking when we had our first child. After two years of marriage, we welcomed our baby daughter, but I didn't keep my promise. Though I did cut back for a while, soon I was drinking every day. This time I told my wife I would stop drinking after our second child was born, and four years later we welcomed another daughter. By this time my wife realized I would never stop, so she stopped complaining and let me drink.

Thinking my wife would never know about my drinking habit, I kept my beer at other people's homes where I could grab a few drinks whenever I wanted. My wife, who was a nurse, quickly figured out my ploy. This time, I promised her I would quit drinking when we bought a house. Our new house was large, providing me many hiding places for my beer. My wife quickly caught on and gave me an ultimatum: I would stop drinking or she would leave me. I completely stopped drinking at the house but continued drinking in secret. Hoping to fool my wife, one day I bought half a case of beer when my wife went to the ballpark. I was sure she would never catch me. However, she came home earlier than expected, saw the case of beer, and left the house, taking the girls with her.

As a last-ditch effort to get clean, I called a rehab center to get into a detox program. They accepted me. I expected to spend two days there but wanted to surprise my family, so I left after twenty-four hours. I stayed sober for four months, but temptation got the best of me. I was drinking more heavily than before. My wife again discovered my drinking and asked for a divorce. When the divorce was granted, I moved out and drank as much as I wanted, except when my daughters visited me. During their visits, whenever I needed a drink, I would drop them off at my parents' so the girls would never know. Because of my drinking, I had two DUIs, but these citations failed to get my attention.

The following Easter, I took my girls to church, but rather than going to the nearby church, I decided to go to the church where my girls wanted to go. That Easter service was a turning point in my life. I felt the preacher was talking to me, and I decided to begin attending this church. The drinking, however, continued, and I would drink on the way to church as well as going home. I kept to myself, avoiding people and church ministries. I came to the end of my rope one weekend when I realized that during that entire weekend, I had consumed over one hundred beers. This was happening every weekend. It was a miracle I didn't suffer from alcohol poisoning.

Suddenly, the Holy Spirit spoke to me. I fell on my knees and prayed earnestly for the Lord to remove my addiction. Destroying the beer I had left, I prayed that Jesus would keep me strong. Like many addicts who fight the battle of addiction, I fell into depression. I knew I needed support. That support came from my dad, who invited me to live with him. Though he still drank, he did not drink around me.

I started to attend a recovery meeting and the Wednesday-night Bible study at our church. At first, I was embarrassed to attend the recovery meeting, but I was comforted because there were so many people there. Our leader admitted he, too, had struggled with addiction, which was comforting. As I attended every week, I made new friends, and before long, I started to help out. I would show up early and stay late.

In the early fall my preacher's message was about salvation through Jesus Christ. One night the preacher revealed that when he was younger, he had a burning conviction that he wasn't saved, and in that moment, he turned his life over to the Lord. I, too, was having those feelings and realized that though I thought I was saved when I was younger, I was not. Early in September 2017, I accepted Jesus Christ as my Savior. Christians are often tempted by Satan to return to the world, and I was no exception. I became actively involved in church ministry. I have been sober for over two years, and to avoid relapsing, I stay strong in God's Word and attend recovery meetings three times a week.

I encourage anyone struggling with addiction to seek help in Jesus Christ. Turn your battles over to Him, and He will give you the strength to overcome your addiction, whatever it may be. Go to your local church, find a recovery meeting, and see what God can do for you and through you. I hope you have received a blessing and encouragement from my story. God bless.

PRESENT

Present ▪

She has gone to church her whole life. Having guy friends who are open and honest about their problems, she has trouble understanding how someone could be addicted to pornography or masturbation. She finds herself in the midst of a sin struggle. She seeks God and finds that He is always present and forgiving.

A t a young age, I accepted Jesus Christ as my Savior. For as long as I can remember, I have been in church. I have always been the type of person who had a plan. My life was precisely planned out, but over the years my plans as well as my desires have changed.

Growing up, I was optimistic for the most part. I could never understand why anyone was grouchy or irritable. Even the worst of my days seemed pretty good. I always kept my head high and was confident in myself, but I remained humble. I knew who I was in Christ, so I was able to walk through life confidently. My parents were very supportive of me. They taught me many things that even now as an adult I still apply to my life. They always taught me to do my very best. If I did, that was enough. They instilled in me that everything we have or are able to do comes from God. Through my parents teaching and living like Christ, God became very real to me. At this point, as a young child, my faith in God was very strong.

In middle school and high school, I was a good girl according to the world's standards. I very rarely got in trouble, and if I did, it was over something silly. I most definitely was not a perfect child since I made mistakes just like any other teenager. I knew that God had a plan and purpose for me, and I knew I wanted to see it fulfilled. When I was in high school, I had several close male friends. One guy, who was very kind and could make almost anyone laugh, was one of my best friends. One evening we attended a party, and our group of friends decided to play the truth-or-dare game. My friend Brian got picked and chose to tell the truth. Some of the guys saw this as a moment to be funny, but I think they did it on purpose to embarrass him.

They asked if he secretly watched porn and masturbated when he was home alone. He looked at me with sad eyes, then looked away and answered yes. The sad part was the fact the one who called him out was struggling with the same thing. The other guys just laughed, and the game continued. Later that night, I received a text from Brian; it was a long message apologizing and telling me how much he hated himself because of the porn and masturbation. He told me he was sorry that I had to find out that way and asked if I would keep praying for him. I encouraged him and told him that I would. Every now and then, I would check up on him to see how he was doing, and each time he reassured me he was doing better. Judging Brian never once crossed my mind; my heart only broke for this friend who was struggling. Brian was the first person I knew who was open and honest with me about his struggles.

Fast-forward to college. During a class taught by an elderly gentleman whose grandson was team-teaching with him, something interesting happened. The grandpa decided that on the last day of this week-long class, his grandson Kyle would teach on his own. Kyle shared his testimony of his eight-year addiction to pornography. His so-called friends were the ones who had introduced it to him. He shared how God saved him and brought him through his addiction. I remember how much I admired him for his bravery and honesty.

I remember thinking, *It would be super hard to marry someone who struggled with pornography.* I never judged him because we all sin, but we just all sin differently. However, I couldn't understand how someone could be addicted to pornography.

Have you ever heard the saying: "Sin will take you further than you ever want to go and keep you longer than you ever want to stay"? One moment of weakness, and I gave into the temptation of masturbation. Although I only did it once, afterward I felt ashamed and disgusted. How could I do something like that? My moment of weakness taught me humility. No one is too good to fall into any temptation. I fell to my knees and begged for God to take my desire to masturbate away. I was open and honest with God about how good it felt, and I told Him that I understood how people could become addicted. I knew that if I didn't do something about it right then, I could soon become addicted, too, even after just one time. Since that moment, by God's grace and my dependence on Him, I have not indulged in it again. It took time for me to get over my shame and guilt. I never thought that masturbation was a sin I was capable of committing, but through this temptation, God has humbled me and has restored me to Him. Through this one-time struggle, God allowed me to understand how easily it could have been to become addicted to this sin, which allowed me to have more compassion for those who have struggled with it.

One year later, I met Logan, and we became close friends. His actions showed me every day how much he cared about me. Although we didn't know at the beginning of our relationship, God was up to something so much bigger than we could have imagined. We sat down one day and had a conversation that was difficult to have. We both shared with each other secrets that we had held on to and never told another soul. He opened up to me about an addiction to pornography that he had struggled with for years. In the moment, I wasn't angry or upset. I asked him if I could pray for him right then and there. I knew the power of prayer in my own life. It was one of the sweetest moments for the two of us.

Over time, I didn't realize how much his problem had affected and hurt me. I would make myself sick just thinking about how many naked girls he had seen over the years. My insecurities grew, and I became worried and jealous any time he was ever around another girl. I always wondered if he was picturing other girls naked or if he liked their bodies better than mine. He opened up to me one day about how he had slipped up and viewed pornography again. Physical pain I can deal with, but when my heart was broken I felt as if I were dying all the time. I became angry with him. I wanted to end the whole relationship.

God graciously reminded me of His mercy and grace toward me. He reminded me of how much He loves me even in the midst of my failures. Remembering my own shame and guilt, I knew Logan probably felt the same way. I, too, had chosen flesh instead of Christ. I came to believe God graciously allowed the two of us to come together so we could share the love of Jesus Christ and experience more understanding and patience for one another. Even though there are times when I still struggle with my insecurities, God has been gracious enough to help me through them and to show more compassion. Afterward, Logan and I chose different paths.

Over the years, I have had my fair share of temptation and trials. But one thing has remained constant: the love of my heavenly Father and Jesus Christ. They have helped me through so many difficult times. Although my life has not gone exactly as I had imagined, one of the biggest lessons I have learned is contentment. God gives me grace in difficult times, and His plans for us are far bigger than we could ever imagine. No matter what, always remember God is working all things out for good for those who choose to love and follow Him. We just have to believe it.

FREEDOM

Freedom •

He is looking to be anyone but himself. After he falls into the bondage of alcoholism and drug addiction, he tries to find a way out by taking his own life. God has other plans.

I was born in Kentucky and moved to Texas when I was about three months old. I was diagnosed with spinal meningitis at ten months of age and stayed in the hospital for about forty-five days. After that, I remained healthy for the rest of my childhood. I am the baby in a family of five siblings. My parents divorced when I was seven. My dad was an abusive alcoholic and died from that disease. He always told my brother, who is two years older than me, to finish his beer and get him another one. We moved to Alabama when I was six, and there I was actively involved in sports year-round.

When I was twelve, I decided I wanted to drink because I thought it would make me look cool to all my friends. I really wanted to impress both them and the older guys in our group. I desired to be anyone but myself, so I started smoking pot at the age of fifteen. Three weeks before I turned sixteen, we moved from Birmingham to a small town about sixty miles north. I was able to easily access the harder drugs like cocaine, meth, medical pills, acid, ecstasy, and psychedelic mushrooms, as well as whatever else I could get. I paid for my habit by selling drugs.

All I wanted was to be wanted by others. When I was younger, I was sexually molested. Because of this experience, I was using drugs and selling drugs, living the life of a drug addict. I finished high school and went to college, but I never finished. I worked in several restaurants at the time, washing dishes and bussing tables. I always ran out of money. I could never get enough of anything: money, drugs, alcohol. I moved back to Birmingham, where I found jobs in the restaurant business that catered to my continued drinking and drug use.

Later, I developed a close relationship with a young lady, and we moved in together. At first, the relationship was successful, but it was based on lying and cheating, which eventually led to our breakup. The trauma of this decision led to my first attempt to kill myself. I ingested close to eighty Clonazepam, hoping to end my life. But God had other plans. After I took the pills, I walked around for several hours. This diminished the effect of the pills to the point that I didn't need to go to the hospital. I was disappointed in myself and felt like a failure because my suicide attempt didn't work. I thought that I couldn't even do that correctly.

After that suicide attempt, my buddy and I decided to travel throughout the United States before we found wives and started our own families. We sold all our possessions and hit the road. We visited Oklahoma, Georgia, South Carolina, and Arkansas. I decided to stay a while in Arkansas, and was fortunate enough to get a job at a restaurant. I had to sleep in my van. During this time, I married a woman I worked with. We had a child together. I attempted to curtail my drug usage, but I failed.

I had been in the restaurant business my whole life. I moved from job to job, continuing to work and advance my skills in food preparation and service. The restaurant industry was an easy way to access drugs and alcohol. This led to my frequent moves, but I got my big chance when I was offered a job as a sous chef. However,

I began working and found the job wasn't what I expected. I became extremely unhappy and mentally depressed.

This was a destructive cycle I had experienced before. I felt as if I could never dig out of the hole I was in, so I decided I would try to commit suicide again. I was serious this time. I decided to take eighty Clonazepam, and I washed the pills down with a fifth of whiskey. I decided to go to the place where I thought my life had started and planned to end it here. My wife and I had married in a pavilion on the side of a large lake. I parked at the top of the hill and started walking down to the pavilion. I was not steady on my feet and stumbled into the lake. I had apparently blacked out momentarily. By the grace of God, when I woke up, I found myself curled up in a ball next to the lake's barrier wall because I was so cold. Leaving the lake, I walked back up the hill to my Explorer.

I was not fit to drive. Because of my condition, it was not surprising I had a wreck. I was stopped by the police and ordered to do a blood alcohol test. The test indicated a high level of alcohol, though below the legal limit. The officer took me to jail, where I was allowed to sober up for a few hours. Fortunately, I was not arrested. My wife, however, refused to come and pick me up from jail because we had a young daughter. My wife was angry and disappointed in me.

Because of the pressure I felt from the people around me, I decided to check myself into an outpatient rehabilitation center. This decision was not for me, but to please all the other people who insisted I needed help. I said I would never use again, and leaving the rehab center, I really and truly meant every word I said. Not surprisingly, twenty-seven days passed, and I got high again.

Life went back to normal. It was not long after this incident that I received an executive chef position at a hotel. They had just lost their chef and were looking for a replacement. Because of the responsibility that comes with being an executive chef and the pressure that goes with it, I was working all the time. Unfortunately, I fell back into the habit of drinking alcohol, using drugs, and selling dope. I was like a juggler trying to keep all the balls in the air. It soon became apparent that I was unable to keep up with this busy life. I had lost all my enthusiasm, and life didn't seem to have meaning anymore.

Family life was not going well at this time, and I decided, for the third time, to end my life. I made careful preparations. I chose to kill myself on my daughter's third birthday. I was afraid that I might go to jail for my decisions, and I couldn't bear for her to see me behind bars. I took a handful of Clonazepam again; this was on top of the ecstasy and weed that were already in my system as well as the other medications that I can't remember. To ensure my success, I retrieved a gun from the bedroom closet and went outside to the back porch so my family wouldn't see me end my life. I put the gun under my chin and pulled the trigger. Because of the number of drugs in my system and the trauma of the bullet passing through my chin, the roof of my mouth, and my skull, I don't remember much of the aftermath of the incident. My wife came out of the house and saw me standing, bleeding profusely. I don't know how, but when the paramedics brought the stretcher, I was able to place myself on the gurney. I was semiconscious on the way to the hospital, but I didn't realize what I had done.

I remained in the hospital for five weeks. Sometime during my stay, my wife informed me that because I had been doing drugs behind her back and lying, she wanted a divorce. I couldn't blame her. I felt the need to return to Alabama to be near my family and attend inpatient rehab in the area. My sister and brother-in-law picked me up from the hospital and drove me to Alabama to an inpatient rehab.

It was a twenty-one-day facility program, and I learned so much important information during my three weeks. This program provided courses on designs for living addiction free. They provided different scenarios of situations we would face in life to help us overcome them to avoid falling into a damaging life again. In a book they provided, there was a chapter called "We Agnostics" that talked about God. I knew there was a God, but when I was doing drugs and alcohol, I thought I *was* God. In this program, they said that either God is everything or nothing. In that moment, I exchanged my fears for faith in God. He gave me the ability to love myself so I can love others like He wants me to. I continue on His path of love today.

I was released from treatment and began changing my life by going to church and following the steps provided in rehab. After the inpatient rehab, my divorce was finalized. I began going to Alcoholics Anonymous two times a day, five or six days a week. I now go to AA at least three times a week, and I call my sponsor every day. I am a living testimony to the saving grace of Jesus Christ.

A mutual friend introduced me to a kind lady. We had never met face-to-face but pursued a friendship through texting and talking on the phone. We decided to meet, and Christmas Day seemed the perfect time for that. Her ex-husband is an alcohol and drug addict. During their married life, she attended programs for spouses whose partners were addicts. Our relationship deepened and we married. She continues to be a supportive and loving wife to me. We now have a very active little girl. We call her our miracle baby for two important reasons: my wife was told she could never have children, and I'm still alive to be a father. I do have a relationship with my oldest daughter, who still lives in Arkansas. I talk to her a couple of times a week, and she spends time with us for weeks during the year.

Have I thought about suicide since my last attempt? Yes, but I reach out and talk to my sponsor about my suicidal thoughts. I stay closely connected to God. Under His guidance, I replace my fears with faith and remind myself every morning to give everything to God. If I struggle with thoughts or worries later in the day, that means I am still trying to control my life, reminding me that I have not fully given it to God for the day. I thank God every day for giving me another chance at life. God has taught me that He doesn't protect *from* the storms but will protect me *in* the storm. Because of God's continual presence in my life, I have been both clean, sober, and forgiven by His grace since April 2011.

■ LOSS

Loss •

She is lost in the loss of a loved one. She watches her child pass from death to life. A staircase accident turns her life around. She finds hope and grace in her heavenly Father's embrace, learning that even in loss, God is enough for her.

Born into a Christian home, I was raised in church my whole life. In August 1994, I attended a Bible-based summer camp in Georgia, where, at the age of fourteen, I was saved. I remember thinking, *I know the verses, I know the Romans Road, I know the plan of salvation ... and I know God can save me. But how can I know that God wants to save me?* The sweet lady helping me during my conviction prayed for me that God would open my eyes to His saving power. The point of salvation for me was when she read me 2 Peter 3:9 (KJV): "The Lord is not slack concerning his promise, as some men count slackness; but is longsuffering to us-ward, not willing that any should perish, but that all should come to repentance."

When she read that verse, before I even said a prayer or a single word, I felt the peace of God enter into my life. Praise God. I accepted Him into my heart and life. He became my personal Savior that day. My life changed forever.

From that point in my life, I had a typical high school and teenage experience. I got my driver's license, had my first crush, got my first job, and eventually graduated high school. Shortly after graduation, I met the man I would marry. As many young couples do, we married quickly. Two months after we met, we decided to get married in December of the same year. Looking back, I realize it probably wasn't the smartest thing I've ever done. I was young and ready to have everything I thought life had promised. In August 1999, I gave birth to my first child, Lucas. He was so perfect, and I was so inexperienced. I had never even babysat before! I had to learn everything. *Everything*. I was so inadequate, but I enjoyed being a mom.

My husband and I, being young and immature, had a few arguments in the next several months—arguments that should have been handled better. I was foolish. When Lucas was only five months old, I left my husband to move to Michigan and live with my mother. My husband filed for divorce, which was granted in 2001. Now it was time for me to grow up. I knew I had to provide for my Lucas, so I reluctantly got my own apartment, found a decent job, and bought a car. We didn't have much, but we were fairly happy. Lucas was silly, adorable, full of life and curiosity. He was a great joy to me.

In October 2002, two months after my son's third birthday, he became very ill. Doctors tried to treat his symptoms for weeks on end. I would administer medicine, and he would feel better for a couple of days, and then all of his symptoms would come back even worse. I was terribly concerned on his final trip to the local ER when he spiked a fever of 106 degrees Fahrenheit and we saw a large mass bulging from his neck. Within an hour the doctors gave me the news that Lucas had leukemia.

I had heard of leukemia, but I didn't know what it meant. The doctors and nurses asked me to sign several papers, and within minutes rushed us to Children's Hospital by ambulance. They began sticking Lucas with needle after needle. They took countless blood samples. There were so many doctors around him, all I could see were his little feet at the end of the examination table. In those minutes I heard the doctors talking, and I was able to put it all together. Leukemia was cancer. My child was actually dying right before my eyes.

Lucas fought hard over the next several months and was able to reach remission after several rounds of chemotherapy. I cannot put into words what it felt like to watch my child suffer that way. But he eventually regained strength and his health was restored.

In the time Lucas was sick, my ex-husband visited us often so he could see him. Because of Lucas's hospitalization, my husband and I were able to talk on a more mature level and found that we had feelings for one another that had never gone away. In August 2003, we remarried and bought a home in Alabama. For a little over a year, we all lived a healthy, normal life. Lucas, cancer-free, played outside, running and jumping like a normal little boy. In September 2004, I gave birth to my second son, Owen. Lucas was a big brother!

We started attending church as a family in November 2004. We loved it. We *needed* it. We were a happy, healthy family of four. In January 2005, things changed. Lucas had a regularly scheduled appointment at the oncologist's office, and we traveled to Birmingham like we did each month to have blood drawn and get a checkup. It was then that they told us the cancer had returned; this time the disease was much more aggressive. Lucas was immediately started on an intense chemotherapy regimen. In April 2005, the doctors discovered that the chemo wasn't working anymore, and Lucas needed a bone marrow transplant. The doctors warned us that he would have to stay in the hospital for an extended time. Lucas was admitted to the hospital and received the lifesaving transplant. I lived with him in the hospital for about eleven weeks before he was able to come home.

During our hospital stay, we were dealt another hard blow.

In May, just a few weeks after Lucas's transplant, my mom had a massive heart attack and died. She was fifty-five years old. I knew her health had been declining, but it came as such a shock. I remember thinking I'd lost part of myself when she died. But truth be told, I barely had time to process her death while dealing with Lucas. Life goes on, and so it did.

Lucas reached remission again in September 2005. He was cancer free! The transplant had worked. We were back to monthly visits to the doctor instead of week- or month-long hospital stays. Lucas's hair was coming back. We were reunited with Owen, who was our hearts' joy. I was able to process the loss of my mother and move forward for the sake of my children. Most importantly, we were able to attend church on a more regular basis. God moved in my heart and my life through my church family and through the preaching of His Word. Our family became closer to each other and to God. I started to realize what it meant to have a personal relationship with Christ.

We had several weeks of normal life. We didn't take one day for granted. But in November 2005, Lucas relapsed again because the cancer was in his spine. From that point, Lucas's health declined rapidly over the next two years. He went through countless chemo treatments and even more radiation treatments. He would go into remission for a couple of months after each treatment, and then he would relapse again. Each time he relapsed, the cancer spread to different parts of his body. Finally, in February 2007, the doctors advised that there were no more treatment options and encouraged us to stop all treatment. The chemo was killing his body and not affecting the cancer in any way. They advised us to stop all medications except those that would keep him pain free and comfortable. They told us to go home and enjoy what time we had left with him. The doctors predicted he had about six months of his life left. So that's what we did. From February until June

2007, we cherished every moment. We took advantage of every minute of energy he had in him. We laughed a lot! And I cried a lot … in private, mostly.

In July 2007, Lucas took a turn for the worse, and we knew the time was getting close. The doctors asked us if we wanted to be admitted to the hospital or let him live his final days at home. I chose to stay in the hospital. The choice is different for every family, I guess. But I wanted my memories of Lucas at home to be happy ones. I didn't want to remember him in his bed, dying. They admitted us to the hospital in early July. A few days into August, Lucas woke me up in the early morning hours. We were not aware he had been rectally bleeding during the night, until we saw his pajamas and sheets that had blood on them. The doctors told us we were down to his last hours. In the last forty-eight hours of his life, I watched the toll death took on my child's body. I sat next to Lucas's bed for three days without sleep, food, or drink. I just sat, watched, waited. Two days later, I lay my head on his bed and closed my eyes to sleep for the first time in days. I intended to rest just a minute. A nurse gently called me to wake up because she believed he had passed away. Lucas had leaned over on top of me and passed from death to life, lying on top of my arm. My first reaction was disbelief. I waited for the nurse to check for a pulse. When she confirmed that he was gone, I lifted Lucas into my arms and held him for the last time. His body was so limp, so lifeless. It was over. We made our phone calls and accepted visitors. We comforted each other. Then we walked out of the hospital with a piece of our hearts missing.

The funeral was a whirlwind of emotions and chaos. So many people. So many comforting condolences. So many flowers! It was not until a couple of months after Lucas's death that I started to really know grief. The first couple of months were hard, obviously. But they were also filled with phone calls, messages, letters, cards, and visitors. I wasn't really alone to process his death for myself. People moved on with their lives, and the phone calls subsided. I started to grieve intensely. I started to feel like I didn't know who I was anymore.

The grief was physically painful for me. I felt that a part of me had died and that I was never going to be of any use to anyone again. I felt that my whole purpose in life was taking care of that child. Now that God had taken him, I truly believed my time was up and God was going to kill me. I anticipated someone murdering me or dying in a car accident. I had the doctors constantly checking me for cancer because I was so sure that God was done with me and my life was over. I think on some deep level I wanted it to be over.

I still had my little Owen, who was two years old at the time of Lucas's passing. I had spent so much time away from him that he and I hadn't bonded. He didn't even know me. I felt rejected by my own son. My family and I couldn't really lean on each other through all of this either. We were all grieving in our own way. We didn't even get along well for a few months. We were just trying to stay alive and make it through. Church family, as much as they tried to be there for me, didn't comfort me at all. Because the truth is, when you've lost someone so close to you, there is nothing that can take that pain away.

In May 2008, almost a year after my son died, God spoke so personally to me that He changed me forever. I was wallowing in grief that had turned into depression. I was feeling downright sorry for myself. Some people told me that it was normal, but I didn't feel normal. I knew I was supposed to have more peace than this. I was a child of God. Where was the peace that passeth all understanding that is mentioned in Philippians 4:7? I didn't even know who I was. I felt my life was like a scattered puzzle, with pieces everywhere, and every time I'd try to pick up the pieces, none of them would fit together. I had lost myself. But God showed me where I was one Sunday morning in May when I faced what I like to call my "staircase accident."

After Sunday school, I had started down the staircase in the front part of the church building just like I had every other Sunday after Sunday school. Before my feet could reach the bottom of the staircase, I missed a step, and my ankle turned and snapped. My foot crumpled beneath me, sending me into a tumbling mess down the steps to the bottom. It wasn't anyone's fault. I had my hands full and was carrying more than I should've been to avoid making a second trip. At first it was quiet. There were only a few people who witnessed the accident. As other Sunday school classes dismissed, foot traffic thickened. People passed by me and asked the same questions over and over: "What happened? Are you okay? Is there anything you need?" I just wanted everyone to leave me alone with some of my dignity intact. After the crowd left, my loyal husband helped me to my one good foot. The next day the doctor diagnosed a pulled tendon. He gave me some minor instructions. The most important thing he told me was to baby the ankle. It would heal, but it was going to take time. My foot stayed tender and sensitive for weeks. Yet God wouldn't let me forget the staircase accident. He spoke great truths to my heart through that healing process.

My Lucas had died. Just like the staircase accident, no one was at fault, not even me. It just happened. Because life happens. But in my grief, I had lost myself. I had allowed myself to be consumed with grief, much like when I was sitting at the bottom of that staircase.

After Lucas's death, people eventually stopped checking on me, leaving me sitting there alone with my wound. I was able to quickly arise from the staircase accident because I had to walk, I had to heal, I had to keep going. But after Lucas's funeral, I totally changed. The person I had been was gone, and I was hopeless. His loss crippled me, keeping me from hope or even strength to carry on. I was bitter from holding in my great sorrow. I chose to be this dejected, worthless woman. My injury became part of God's transforming power. As my ankle slowly healed, God was causing a transforming healing in my heart. Just like my injured ankle went through different stages of healing, my heart also had to go through different stages of healing. Slowly but surely, God renewed my heart as well as my life. There are scars that reveal God's handiwork in my life. Even though my life has been transformed, there are still times of pain and sorrow. Through my journey, other aches and bruises have been revealed that I didn't even know were there. Healing doesn't happen overnight.

For a long period I chose to wallow and whine in self-pity. I felt defeated and crippled from the battle of trying to save Lucas. God helped me to realize that these feelings were a selfish illusion. There was strength available with His help to stand up and continue with my life. I have to admit it was a painful but not hopeless journey. Healing begins with finding the will to *be* healed. As I have been writing this, I have been praying that the message "Jesus is enough" will impact the life of my readers.

The death of Lucas is just one story of loss from my life. Most recently I've been through the great loss of seeing my sister fall under the bondage of addiction. My sister, my best friend from the time I was born, has completely changed. She is not the person I used to know. I cannot be close to her because she has lied and manipulated and given in to so much substance abuse that she has turned into a person I don't want to know. I've witnessed her addiction cause physical sickness, mental dysfunction, abusive relationships, and most recently, homelessness. My sweet Sissy, the one I strived to emulate when I was younger, is gone. Once again God is helping me face the grief of losing someone that has been such a huge part of my life.

Because of God, I remember the lessons I have learned. Loss is a part of life. I've lost both parents and my grandparents. I've lost jobs, homes, cars, and friends. There are many different types of loss in life. I think that the most valuable lesson God has allowed me to learn is that through any loss, He is always enough. I can choose to embrace the loss and let it mold me and change me to be more like Christ, or I can wallow in the self-pity, claiming to be handicapped and choosing to be a victim.

For me it's sometimes been easy to put too much value on the things and the people in my life. I've begun to think they are what make me who I am. Through each loss I've experienced, however, God has revealed to me that people and possessions are not what makes us who we are. Before I am a child, mother, wife, sister, friend, employee, homeowner, college dropout, or anything else, I am *His* child, a child of the King. So when I experience loss, although it can be quite painful, I don't have to feel lost. I am determined by *Whose* I am. I am His. He is enough.

FAITHFUL

Faithful •

*Experiencing his parents' divorce at an early age, it is easy for him to
find comfort in alcohol and drugs. Alcohol and drugs make others like
him, but eventually lead him to being homeless. Treatment centers
and jail time, marriage and a child, nothing can change him. The
only change that lasts comes when he meets a faithful Father.*

I grew up in a small town in Alabama. My mother and father
were divorced when I was very young, so I do not remember
them being married. My earliest memories occurred after my
father married my stepmother. My father was an electrician. He
worked very hard, and I remember him going to work every day
and working long hours. My father also drank every day; I never
remember a time when he wasn't drinking. My mother was the
party drinker. After my parents divorced, she married a man who
worked as a boat salesman. Because mother and my stepfather
lived near a large lake, they frequently threw parties or attended
parties on the weekends.

I took my first drink when I was thirteen years old. My parents'
divorce decree gave custody to my father, but I spent my summers
with my mother. I was at my mother's house when they were
having a party for some friends who were getting married. I had
heard it said alcohol does something to someone who drinks it.
I will never forget the way it made me feel. It transformed me: I

was no longer the short, overweight, shy kid no one liked. All of a sudden, after a few drinks, I was completely changed: people liked me, I could sing, I could dance, I could talk to girls. That Mazda in the driveway became a Maserati. I was the center of attention that night.

I remember as I was mixing my second drink, my mother came in and caught me. She told me to mix it with Sprite so I wouldn't be as sick in the morning. Mother's advice didn't work. The next morning, I was as sick as I have ever been. As I lay on the bathroom floor throwing up, I remember thinking, *Last night was awesome.* Other than being sick, there were no real consequences for what I had done. I drank as often as I could from that point forward, except when I stayed with my father. He would have sent me to a treatment center if he caught me drinking.

When my father finally realized that I was drinking heavily, he said he couldn't deal with my behavior and grounded me. My drinking eventually led to my use of harder drugs, which caused lots of trouble. When I turned sixteen and got my first car, drinking and harder drugs became much easier. Owning a car enabled me to stay away from the house for long periods of time. When I came home late, my dad would be asleep and wouldn't realize I was drunk. This became an almost daily occurrence.

One Friday night, I went out drinking and didn't come home for several weeks. I stayed in my car or with a friend during this time. I would drink and stay drunk for days. Also, at this time, I got heavily into drugs, specifically marijuana and methamphetamines. My dad had me arrested for unauthorized use of a vehicle; this was the first of many trips to jail. I was put on juvenile probation and eventually was sent to my first treatment center. I quickly learned what to say and how to act to make the counselors happy. Since there was no set time to remain in treatment, they let me go when they felt I was ready to be discharged.

I went to treatment the second time as an inpatient. They had their own school system, enabling me to attend high school. Once again, I completed treatment with flying colors, only to drink and use meth again shortly after. I quit using all the drugs except meth, to which I was completely addicted. I realized I had an overwhelming problem and tried to do everything humanly possible to get sober. When I graduated high school, I joined the Marine Corps, thinking the structure would help keep me sober. Unfortunately, before I completed boot camp, I was discharged for getting high. I had a few brief periods of sobriety, but they never lasted long.

At age nineteen, I found myself homeless for the first time. I ended up in jail for several months. This was enough time to get my mind clear. When I got out, I moved in with my brother and got a good job with the electrical contractor my dad and brother had worked for. I started going to church for the first time in my life. I was in church every time the doors were open. It was like I could not get enough. One Wednesday night, I don't remember what the preacher was preaching. I only remember that when I left, I couldn't stop crying. I got home and called the preacher, who was a recovering addict himself, and he led me to the Lord that night over the telephone. Kneeling down on the floor of my brother's living room, I gave my life to the Lord.

I would love to tell you that I never drank or used again, but that was not the way it worked for me. I thought when I got saved everything would be good. I thought the desire to drink and use would just go away. I stopped going to church. I stopped reading my Bible. I thought I was done. I thought I had finished the race. Little did I know that was just the beginning.

I eventually used again. When this happened, I thought salvation didn't work for me. I thought I was such a bad person and so far gone even God couldn't help me. Something changed inside of me when I got saved. Until salvation, the things I was doing didn't really bother me. I thought I was only hurting myself. I just wanted everyone to leave me alone and let me get high. After salvation, I felt terrible every time I used. This made me use more to cover up those feelings. The more I used, the worse I felt. The worse I felt, the more I used. It was an endless cycle.

I knew I had to find a way to get clean or I was going to die. I tried the Marine Corps again. When you arrive at Parris Island, they drug test you. However, the results take time to process, so I continued on with training. Once they received the drug test results, I was released from boot camp and sent home. When I returned home, I was reacquainted with a young lady I had dated in high school. We dated for a while and then decided to get married. I thought surely getting married would make me grow up and be a man. When that didn't work, I became angry with my wife and drank even more.

I thought having a child would surely make me grow up and be the man God intended me to be. My daughter was the most beautiful thing I had ever seen. I knew real love for the first time in my life the very first time I saw her. Every time I drank or used, all I could think was, "What kind of man can't stay sober for his daughter?" The simple truth is treatment wasn't enough, boot camp wasn't enough, my wife was not enough, and even my daughter wasn't enough to keep me sober. I hit my all-time low. After four short years of marriage, we got a divorce. Things quickly got worse. I lost my job, was evicted from several different homes, and found myself living with my mother.

Years went by, and things continually got worse. I ended up in a faith-based treatment center, where I started to develop a relationship with God again. When I got out of the treatment center, I went back to my old ways. I stopped reading my Bible and going to church and eventually found myself worse off than I had ever been. God was trying to draw me closer to Him, but I kept running away. Every time I would drink or use, I would end up in jail again. I remember sitting on my mom's back porch hearing the church bell at the local church on Sunday morning. I remember thinking I should go, and perhaps I could find the solution there. But I would always talk myself out of it, thinking I was too far gone. I needed to get cleaned up first. I never could quite get there on my own. Unfortunately, after I lived with my mom for a couple of years, she asked me to leave.

Several long years later, I was still at rock bottom. I got stopped for a bad tag one night. By the time the traffic stop was over, I had been charged with three felonies and a misdemeanor. Two weeks later I was given another felony. Shortly after this, God sent six angels—county police officers—into the house where I was staying. The police officers raided the home and put everyone on the ground. Lying on the floor of the nastiest house you can imagine, I cried out to God, "Please help me!" and He did! I thought I had to get cleaned up for God. Turns out, I had to get God to get cleaned up. I went to see my drug court officer, and for the first time, I was completely honest with another human being. I told her I couldn't stay clean on my own. I needed help.

In November 2014, I entered a treatment center for the last time. I have not taken a drink or used a drug since. I went from treatment to a halfway house, where I was introduced to Alcoholics Anonymous. The Twelve Steps did for me what I believe God meant for them to do. The twelfth step says that having had a spiritual awakening as a result of these steps, we try to carry this message to other alcoholics who still suffer. Since then, God has seen fit to put my whole life back together one piece at a time. I stayed in the halfway house for a year. I got a job, bought a car, and bought a travel camper, which I lived in for two years. I started visiting my daughter, who lived in my hometown, on a regular basis. I had been out of her life for fourteen years. We had to get to know each other again. We started going to church on the Sundays I was home to visit. My wife had gotten involved in a recovery ministry at church, and I started going with her. I got as involved as I could get with church and the recovery ministry.

God started calling me back to my hometown to get more involved with church and a recovery ministry. I was scared to go back because I was afraid I would go back to my old ways. Eventually, I took a leap of faith. I rented a trailer, hooked it to my camper, and went back to town. I was earning almost half of what I was used to making and had more bills. I was scared, but I kept doing what God asked me to do, and He kept blessing me. I got a raise at my job and eventually got a job offer at the company I originally worked. I did not think they would ever consider giving me another chance. Now I am a field superintendent in charge of multimillion-dollar projects.

In December 2018, my wife and I were remarried. After fourteen years of being divorced, God saw fit to give us another chance. After I lived homeless for seven years, sleeping under bridges or wherever I could find a spot, God gave me my wife back and allowed us to buy our first home together. Since then, God has allowed us to lead the recovery ministry and the jail ministry at our church. We use our story to help others who struggle with the same things we experienced. We have been able to help needy couples and addicts. I do not say all this to brag about myself. The very best I could do on my own was to end up hopelessly addicted to drugs and homeless. I tried everything I knew, from a twenty-one-day treatment center to boot camp to yearlong faith-based treatment centers. The only thing that ever made a difference was a real relationship with God. Jesus says in John 10:10 (KJV): "The thief cometh not, but for to steal, and to kill, and to destroy: I am come that they might have life, and that they might have it more abundantly." This has been my life verse. If I had sat down and written out what I wanted out of my life, I would have sold myself way short. Praise God for second chances and an abundant life.

IDENTITY

Identity ▪

She identifies herself with all people have said or done to her. She loses herself
along the way only to read stories that lead her to her Redeemer. Through
all of the heartache and pain, she finds that her identity is in Christ alone.

My name is Elizabeth Kathryn Wells. I was raised in church and had a wonderful home life. My parents loved and supported my brother and me. They instilled in us that we could do anything we put our minds to. We spent the holidays at my maternal grandparents' house. At that time, we weren't as close to my paternal grandparents. Throughout elementary school, I always felt so alone. Although I had many friends, I never had that one best friend that I could talk to about anything. It seemed like I was everyone's friend but realized they weren't mine. I longed to be loved and accepted by others. When it seemed like others didn't love or accept me, I felt so ashamed, rejected, and hurt. Why didn't anyone want me?

Around the age of eight my life changed forever. We were all in the car with my mom's family on the way back to my aunt's house after we went out to eat. In one moment, life as I knew it changed. I was in the back seat with my cousins and grandma. We were all playing and talking, and the topic of pressure points came up. I reached up and pinched the back of my grandpa's arm to show him that it was a pressure point, and, in one instant, he reached around and pinched me all on the inside of my legs and arms. I don't remember anything else until we were back at my aunt's house.

Years later, my mom told me that she thinks I was crying, and it seemed like we couldn't get to my aunt's house fast enough to get me out of the car to see if I was okay. However, she, too, had blocked out most of this day. I don't remember crying or reacting in any way. I remember being inside with my brother and cousins, afraid of what was going to happen as we watched the adults outside the window. The next thing I remember we were at home and my mom was taking pictures of the bruises on my legs and arms. I remember feeling paralyzed by fear as Mom took the photos, and I asked why she was taking them. Would my grandpa go to jail for this? The pictures were for proof that my grandpa had pinched me and left bruises on my body. Mom took photos because she wanted proof in case my parents wanted to get a restraining order against him. My grandpa refused to accept responsibility. We tried mending the relationship with my grandparents, but it didn't work out until fifteen years later because my grandpa wasn't willing to change.

Every single day since that day, I lived in fear, fear of my grandpa showing up at my house, fear that he would hurt me again. I was angry for years. I wished that he was dead so I could have a relationship with my grandma. Years went by, and it seemed like I was always looking over my shoulder. I hated that this was how I had to live my life. Would I run into him at the store? Would he show up at my school? What would he do to me? What would he say? Fear permeated my life. It suffocated me along with the anger I had toward him. Why didn't he want to change so we could be a family again? How could he just walk away from us? Why didn't he pursue a relationship with me? I remember telling my mom one time that you can be family by blood yet not actually love a family member. I was numb. I continued to long for the day he would

FOR THE ONE ■

die. The closest grandparents I knew had rejected me. How was I supposed to trust anyone ever again?

Throughout middle school I was lost, trying to find my way. I was searching for people, besides my parents and brother, who would love me. I was different from everyone else. I didn't jump from one guy to the next guy every week. I didn't have the mouth of a sailor. I didn't gossip about everyone. I knew God's Word, and I was good at using it to show others how they were living was wrong compared to God's truth. I always shared His truth from a place of love, but looking back, my approach was not very Christlike.

Again, I was friends with everyone, and everyone could always count on me to be there for them, but I was always looking for someone to fill that emptiness I felt inside. I longed for the day a guy was interested in me instead of interested in all my friends. During this time in my life, I remember hearing a message at church that sent my heart racing. I knew I needed to talk to someone. I talked to my Sunday school teacher, and she led me through Romans Road and had me repeat a prayer after her. I did. Immediately, I felt relief. However, nothing really changed. My heart was still so prideful.

In freshman year of high school, a group of older girls took me under their wings, and I felt great. I finally felt loved, but even then, I still felt so alone. I would be sitting in the middle of church surrounded by people I knew and feel completely alone. I would be surrounded by people at school who were my friends and I feel empty, alone. After freshman year, I switched schools. I hated the move. I begged to go back to my old school. I begged God for help and for friends. Eventually, I accepted that this was where I needed to be if I wanted to go to college for sports. In high school, I excelled in track and field.

I wasn't a typical high school student. I didn't drink. I didn't go to parties. I didn't have a bunch of boyfriends. I didn't cuss. People would always ask me why I didn't go to parties or anything like that. My answer was always the same: I didn't want to damage my testimony. I was actively involved in church. I was always sharing about God, and if I went to those parties or drank alcohol, what would others think about me? I was supposed to be representing God; I couldn't do that stuff. Yet in my heart I was so angry. I was angry that I never had friends who were as close to me as they were to everyone else. I was angry because I felt unlovable. All my friends would have best friends, and they would get asked out by guys, but I never was. I would do all the right things. I would say all the right stuff. I would go on mission trips and serve in church, and yet, I was so empty, so alone. I knew I was doing all the *right* things, but I always seemed to fall short.

During my sophomore year of high school, I started having severe pain in my ribs in addition to stomach issues. I ignored these symptoms and continued competing in track and field, throwing the javelin. I was really good at this sport and won state medals. However, my accomplishments didn't fill my emptiness. My good works didn't fill my emptiness. My friends didn't fill my emptiness. My rib pain and stomach issues continued to get worse.

Between my sophomore and junior years of high school, my friend and I got into an argument. I was at my friend Avery's house with her cousin. Avery's cousin wanted to roll my other friend Mellie's house with toilet paper. She was friends with her brother. I remember texting Mellie, asking if her brother would be home. My question upset her, and she started asking me why. Well, Avery's cousin didn't want me to tell her, so I didn't.

It caused a big issue. I don't remember everything that was said, but I do remember what she said to me on the phone. Let me explain: at this point in my life, I was very set in my ways, and anyone who knew me knew that I didn't want to kiss a guy until the day I got married. I wanted to save my first kiss for the man

I would spend the rest of my life with. My friend Mellie knew this, and on the phone that day, she accused me of being a lesbian because I didn't want to kiss a guy until the day I got married. It *crushed* me. I remember hanging up the phone with her and calling my mom immediately after.

I was so heartbroken. How could anyone ever think that about me? One of my closest friends had just destroyed me. I never wanted anyone to ever think that about me again. I stopped telling my friends I loved them. I stopped hugging my friends. I filtered everything through the lie she told me, thinking about what others would say or think if I did this or that. I was incredibly fearful that others thought that about me, too, and it wasn't even the truth. At this time, I started living in complete fear of what others thought about me. I repressed everything in fear that someone might think or say something about me that wasn't true. I was miserable. I let that lie destroy me. I even went against my own convictions and kissed a guy to prove that I wasn't what she said I was, even though I knew the truth. For years, I struggled with what she had said to me. How would I ever recover? Not only that, but I wouldn't tell anyone about this because of the fear that they might think the same thing. I was miserable and completely lonely. I let what one person said about me keep me in bondage for more than five years. After that, I felt like I just existed. I still wanted others to love and accept me, but I never wanted to get hurt again. I was numb.

During my senior year of high school, I accepted scholarships to be the mascot and to throw javelin for the track team at a university in Alabama. The summer of 2013, before moving to college, I had my gallbladder removed. The pain and sickness never left; it only got worse. I visited many doctors, but no one had answers. I was miserable my entire freshman year of college. I was constantly sick, so I couldn't even enjoy being on the track team or being the mascot. After my freshman year, I decided to transfer to Virginia for college. I was sick and in so much pain that I could not even walk to my classes. Two months into my sophomore year of college, I moved back home and was able to transfer my classes online.

In 2015, after I moved back home, we went to the doctor, and she diagnosed me with depression. I figured I had been depressed for a while, but when someone diagnoses you with it, it's a shocking realization. I can remember before that moment I would experience times when I would be driving, and a thought would pop into my mind: *What would happen if I just missed this turn?* It happened more often than I care to admit. I can remember thinking, *What would happen if I wasn't here anymore? Would anyone actually miss me?* During this time, my parents were so incredibly supportive but never knew the depths of the pain I felt. I never really told them or let them help me. I was cared for and loved so much. I was in church every Sunday and reading my Bible. I was volunteering in a couple of ministries.

No one would have ever guessed I was not only completely miserable but also in agonizing pain. I wouldn't let anyone into my life. My friends and acquaintances never knew the extent of my struggle. I hid behind a mask, and I was good at it. I identified with my pain. Yes, it was awful, but it was also comfortable. It was the perfect excuse for everything. It allowed me to simply exist without having any responsibilities. Once the doctor diagnosed me with depression, I dug into God's Word like never before. The Bible is what brought me out of that depression. I only had to stay on medication for four months. I was effectively going to school online at the time and deeply involved in the church.

In 2015, I started a full-time internship while continuing to volunteer at church and going to school full time. My mom told me that I should write a book. Within a year, following her suggestion, I wrote a sixty-day devotional book that I self-published in 2016. Life was successful on the outside, but I was still alone and miserable on the inside. It took everything in me to get out of bed each day and show up to work. After the internship ended, I realized I couldn't hold a job because of my pain and sickness. My parents and I went to Vanderbilt University Hospital in Tennessee to try to find answers. We talked to so many doctors there, but again no one had any answers. The only answer they seemed to have was they had no idea what was wrong with me. The pain center did three intercostal nerve blocks that didn't touch the pain I was experiencing. After that, we started discussing the Mayo Clinic in Minnesota. In 2017, we spent two weeks at the Mayo Clinic seeing more than ten doctors who still had no answers or diagnoses for us. We felt completely defeated, yet I kept holding on to God's Word. I accepted this pain and sickness as a gift from God. I thought it was His way of keeping me humble. I thought it was His way of inviting me into a deeper relationship with Him.

Once we got back home, my mom had a friend who used Young Living essential oils. We were at the end of our options. Mom purchased a starter kit of oils and came into my room, telling me I was going to use these oils whether I liked it or not. I spread the oils over my ribs, and for the first time in seven years, I slept through the night comfortably. It was a miracle. About a year later, I met someone whom God used as a catalyst to help heal my body. She started speaking truth to me that I didn't even believe about myself. She refused to believe that this was the life God had for me and dared me to believe God had more in store for me. With the help of that friend, I started eating better and believing that God had a greater plan for my life. I also found a chiropractor who, along with his wife, God used to transform my life so that one day I would be willing to let go of the pain and sickness for God to heal me.

At the end of 2017, I started attending a program at church that helped me overcome the hurts that I had experienced with my grandparents and friends. I went to counseling about the fear that

I was living with because I was terrified to stay in my house alone. My counselor told me, "Elizabeth, you are no longer that eight-year-old little girl. You are a grown woman who can stand up for herself." I told my counselor that I wanted to make peace with my grandparents because I was tired of living in fear. I started praying that if it was God's will to mend that relationship, He would open the door. In March 2018, my maternal grandma asked us all to go to dinner together, and for the first time I felt at peace with seeing my grandpa. It had been more than ten years. I told my grandpa that I loved him despite my earlier fear and anger. Never in my life did I think that day would happen. I once looked more forward to his death than I did reconciliation. Now, we started mending our relationship and going out to eat together. I still didn't want them at my house because I wanted to meet them on my own terms, where I could get away if needed. It was also during this time that I started collecting testimonies for my new book, the book you are holding in your hand. Story after story landed in my inbox. I started reading, and my heart crumbled. My head would fall into my hands as tears fell down my face and onto my keyboard. Paragraph after paragraph of individuals pouring their hearts out to me. Stories that have never been told, details that only their spouses knew, and shared memories that they wish they could forget. However, they were willing to share if it could help one person who might be going through the same thing or have a similar story.

My mind couldn't comprehend it though. How could someone go through such traumatic realities and then believe in God? How could they trust God when they had experienced such terrible things? I have been in church my entire life. I knew the Bible from front to back and knew all the stories throughout the Book. Yet, this didn't make sense to me. I knew about God's love, and I knew about His truth. I had even written a sixty-day devotional book that talked about God and His Word. I'd been overseas and stateside on mission trips. I thought I knew everything there was to know.

After each story I read, I wondered, *How could someone go through awful realities and believe in God?* Months went by, and the question stirred in my soul. How did this not make sense to me? I knew all about God, yet my heart couldn't comprehend someone trusting a sovereign God after experiencing such awful things. God was using testimonies I had never heard to reveal my disbelief in Him.

On a late July night in 2018 in a Wednesday Bible study, surrounded by teenagers from the small group I led, the Holy Spirit convicted my soul. The pastor that night said, "Paul's conversion was not just a moment; it was a life-changing experience." I knew in that moment that I was lost and on my way to hell. It didn't matter if I grew up in church, led people to the Lord, knew the Bible front to back, went on mission trips, or lived the Christian life. I was lost. Our pastor always reminds us that we have to get lost before we can get saved. That statement never made sense to me until that night. Before that night, I thought my sins weren't as bad as everyone else's. I thought because I was a *good girl*, that was enough, but it wasn't. I sat there worried about what people would think of me. I had lived the Christian life and done all the right things. No one would have guessed that I wasn't saved. My flesh was fighting hard not to surrender to God. I got up, grabbed a friend of mine, and left the room. I needed someone to tell me what I had known for years but only had been between God and me. I tried to make sense of the conviction I was feeling. But no head knowledge will ever be able to reason with a sovereign God. I knew what I needed to do. I fell to my knees and repented of my sins. That night I accepted Jesus Christ as my personal Lord and Savior. Early in August 2018, I was baptized.

I had never completely recovered from my rib and stomach pain, although the essential oils brought much relief. In October 2018, I was to accompany my aunt on her business trip to Hawaii. As I drove to her house, God met me on Interstate 65. My anxiety began to take over. I was worried about the flight since the pain in my ribs and my stomach issues continued to bother me. In that moment, it seemed as if the Holy Spirit whispered to me. He seemed to offer to take my pain and sickness from me completely if I were willing to let go of it. As tears fell down my face, I surrendered the pain and sickness to God, and in that moment, my pain was gone.

I boarded a plane with my aunt to Kauai, Hawaii. That week, I went on ATV rides and went deep-sea fishing, hiking, and sailing on a boat around the Nā Pali Coast. Over the past ten years of my life, I was not even able to go on road trips with my parents because I would become extremely nauseous and experience excruciating pain. Here I was in Hawaii, feeling like a completely new person. I was living proof of God's promise to provide all of our needs. Up until this point, I was hiding my true self to please everyone else. I even identified myself with my pain and sickness, using them as a crutch to prevent me from reaching my full potential in Christ. I put on a mask, fearing that no one would love the real me. Trying to earn God's love and the love of others, I thought that doing all the right things would be enough. Working for love or acceptance is easy because it makes you feel you are in control. Surrendering to God, however, means giving yourself completely to Him in faith. God then will give you the gift of salvation provided for you through the sacrifice of the Lamb of God, Jesus Christ.

God dares us to remove our masks. He calls us to live all in with Him and love others with a reckless love. He wants us to share our stories for those experiencing what we have already been through. We are called to share what God has done for us, and that is the purpose of this book. In my case, God has taken me from a life of longing to be loved to a place of being known and loved unconditionally. God has shown me He is my Savior, Father, Redeemer, refuge, and strength. He is the great I AM. He is mine and I am His. I can be boldly myself in Christ because the Holy Spirit lives in and through me. He is my identity, and His Word tells me who I am in Him. All this is available to everyone who will accept Him as their Lord and Savior. Though our sins cling to us, turning to Christ can set us free. His Word can also tell you who you are in Him if you will only accept Him as your Lord and Savior, repenting of your sins and turning to Him. When you become a born-again believer, the only thing that defines you is Jesus Christ.

What the individuals in this book didn't know at the time I interviewed them was that I myself was lost. Each individual shared their story, hoping that one person might come to the truth of Jesus Christ. I myself was broken, and these stories convinced me that I was hopelessly lost without Jesus. I knew all about Him in my head, not in my heart. We share our deepest vulnerabilities and flaws so that you, the reader, *the one*, will come to know Jesus Christ as your personal Lord and Savior too. He loves you, and He created you for more than just being His creation. He wants you to be His child. Each story has a beginning and end, but the middle is where we get the chance to live with Christ on this side of heaven if we accept Him. I can't wait to see Him in the end. I hope to see you there too.

JUST ONE

Just One ▪

One moment. One choice. One love. One God.

> Everything meant something
> And nothing without purpose
> Everything I've been through
> No, none of it was worthless
> So I run and I run
> Hoping to finish the race
> Watching where I'm going
> But looking to Your face
> I may show up to the finish line
> With bandages and scrapes
> But that won't matter to me
> As I collapse into Your embrace
>
> —Charity

E very story told in this book has a purpose. The good, the bad, and the ugly, each story is told for you, the one reading each page, the one with tears streaming down their face, and the one who can only whisper the words, "Me too." You are not alone. We share these stories for you today. We desire to share the hope of Jesus Christ as well as the stories that often go untold. Opening up our hearts, we pray our stories give you the courage to accept Jesus Christ and follow Him, knowing that everything that has happened or that will happen, God can and will use for good for those who love Him and ultimately, for His glory.

Now that you have read these stories of addiction, loss, abuse, unbelief, and miracles, I want you to know that you are not alone in this world. There is someone in this world who may not have the exact story you do but can directly relate to at least one part of your story. Life has a way of leading us to a place where we lose ourselves, whether it be in people, drugs, alcohol, pornography, homelessness, masturbation, loss, or whatever else. We all have our own scars. Each individual who shared their story in this book found a loving, gracious Savior who met them at the most desperate place of their lives. They didn't have to get their lives together before Jesus loved them. They didn't have to follow all the rules or know all the Bible verses. They didn't have to have a perfect family or a clean track record. God just wanted them in their brokenness and lost identities. He had for them a gift of redemption.

We all have tried to fix our problems. Yet many of us found ourselves still crying out for more. We desperately sought something or someone that would love us in our most wretched state. We all tried to run and escape the problems of life, only to find they were right there waiting for us when we ran out of escapes. We get it. It's hard to believe that someone could love us right where we are. Yet if you were to ask any of the individuals in this book, they would say that putting our faith in Jesus Christ was worth all the anguish and heartache we experienced.

No, life isn't rainbows and butterflies. Every day isn't easy, and we still face temptations and trials. But now we have a Savior in heaven who sent His Holy Spirit to comfort us and help us through every single moment of every single day. Just by admitting we were sinners, believing that Jesus died on the cross for our sins, and confessing that He conquered death by rising again on the third day, we are given the gift of eternal life through Jesus Christ. Are you ready to find your identity in the comfort of a heavenly Father who loves you unconditionally?

Romans Road
The Steps to Salvation

1. Recognize that you are a sinner.
   a. Psalm 51(KJV): "Behold, I was shapen in iniquity; and in sin did my mother conceive me."
   b. Isaiah 64:6 (KJV): "But we are all as an unclean thing, and all our righteousnesses are as filthy rags; and we all do fade as a leaf; and our iniquities, like the wind, have taken us away."
   c. Romans 3:23 (KJV): "For all have sinned, and come short of the glory of God."

2. Believe that Jesus Christ died on the cross for your sins.
   a. John 3:16 (KJV): "For God so loved the world, that he gave his only begotten Son, that whosoever believeth in him should not perish, but have everlasting life."
   b. Romans 5:8 (KJV): "But God commendeth his love toward us, in that, while we were yet sinners, Christ died for us."
   c. Second Peter 3:9 (KJV): "The Lord is not slack concerning his promise, as some men count slackness; but is longsuffering to us-ward, not willing that any should perish, but that all should come to repentance."

3. Repent of your sins.
   a. Romans 6:23 (KJV): "For the wages of sin is death; but the gift of God is eternal life through Jesus Christ our Lord."

4. Confess that Jesus Christ is Lord and that He died on the cross for our sins and rose again three days later, overcoming death.
   a. Romans 10:9–10 (KJV): "That if thou shalt confess with thy mouth the Lord Jesus, and shalt believe in thine heart

that God hath raised him from the dead, thou shalt be saved. For with the heart man believeth unto righteousness; and with the mouth confession is made unto salvation."

b. Romans 10:13 (KJV): "For whosoever shall call upon the name of the Lord shall be saved."